Notes on the History of Tong from the Parish Books.

Volume 2

The Third Note Book

of

John Ernest Auden

Vicar of Tong, 1896 - 1913

Published by arima publishing

www.arimapublishing.com

ISBN 1-84549-010-X

Printed and bound in the United Kingdom

Typeset in Palatino 10/16

arima publishing
ASK House, Northgate Avenue
Bury St Edmunds, Suffolk IP32 6BB
t: (+44) 01284 700321

www.arimapublishing.com

Introduction

John Auden was vicar of Tong in Shropshire from 1896-1913. His first two notebooks (Volume 1 in this series) gave us his notes on the history of the parish of Tong and its people from the fourteenth century to the beginning of the twentieth century.

In calling this second volume 'Auden's History of Tong' I am well aware that Auden would have been quick to respond that these are just notes, and in the case of this volume very *rough* notes, only, and far from a full blown 'History'. He has, however, in this his third notebook supplied such an interesting and informed connecting narrative for his fascinating selections from the Registers and the Churchwardens' Accounts and other documents, which he found in the church chest then in use, that we can appropriately call it 'Auden's History'. With these selections from the records those interested in local history have here easy access to some of the original documents, the raw material of history. They provide a varied and often vivid picture of life in Tong from 1630 to the end of the nineteenth century; here we see the life and work of the villagers, as well as of the powerful and mighty who lived in the castle.

Twice as many people lived in Tong then as now. The owners of Tong Castle employed many of the villagers to maintain the castle and estate. The Churchwardens were not only responsible for the repair of the church and the maintenance of the graveyard, but also for the care of the poor and indeed most of the regulation of the inhabitants' daily life. Being a Churchwarden was an onerous task, indeed in some parishes people paid a substantial fine to be released from it. Their accounts give us a valuable glimpse into the life of the village from 1630, including the ravages of the Civil War. When the Civil War was over, Charles II was particularly grateful to those from Tong who sheltered him after the Battle of Worcester, and when he was hiding in the oak at Boscobel.

Tong has changed. The castle became a dangerous ruin and had to be blown up in 1954. All the remaining documents from the Tong Church chests are held now in the safe keeping of Shropshire Archives in Shrewsbury. The Tong Cup mentioned in the notebooks is now securely displayed in Lichfield Cathedral.

In copying these notes I have kept to the quite remarkable assortment of spellings in the original documents, although this gave the computer considerable hiccups. Headings and dates have been highlighted for clarity. Apart from a very few footnotes of my own in square brackets [like this], the footnotes are all those of John Auden himself. A glossary has been added to make the notes more easily accessible and intelligible, and I have included a brief biography of Auden. I am very grateful to those who have allowed me to use their pictures and photos of Tong, especially to John R. L. Smith and Christopher Frost. Particular thanks go to my good friends in Tong for all their cheerful assistance, and to Richard Franklin and his staff at Arima Publishing for their thoughtful help. I would also like to thank my husband for all his valuable support, advice and time in producing this book.

Joyce Frost
December 2004

Glossary

Acre　　　　　4,840 square yards.

Apparitor　　　A man who brought summonses to appear in
(Parritor)　　　civil or ecclesiastical courts. See also under 1667.

Apprentice-　　Many children would be apprenticed voluntar-
ship　　　　　ily to learn a trade, but pauper children and il-
　　　　　　　　legitimate children were a charge upon the par-
　　　　　　　　ish and so were bound by deed indented (in-
　　　　　　　　denture) to a tradesman or anyone, preferably
　　　　　　　　outside the parish to prevent any further ex-
　　　　　　　　pense to the parish.

Artificial　　　The coat of Arms of 1814 on the church north
Stone　　　　wall is made of Coade Ware, an artificial stone
　　　　　　　　invented by Mrs. Coade about 1769.

Beating the　　To trace out and establish the boundaries of a
bounds　　　　parish by formally walking around them. See
　　　　　　　　especially under 1718.

Benevolence　　A forced loan or contribution exacted by the
　　　　　　　　king from his subjects.

Brief (breif)　　A letter from the authorities commending a
　　　　　　　　charitable appeal and for a collection to be made
　　　　　　　　in churches. See list of briefs at the end of the
　　　　　　　　notebooks. Beggars, who were clearly incapable
　　　　　　　　of working, were given a licence (or brief as
　　　　　　　　stated in the accounts) by magistrates after 1530,
　　　　　　　　which entitled them to beg and prevented their
　　　　　　　　being whipped.

Burgage croft A rented plot.

Constable This post has existed since the 13th century. Constables were responsible for law and order in the parish and also in the early days for collecting quarter money.

Court Baron An assembly of freehold tenants under a lord.

Court Leet A court held in the manor before the lord or his steward.

Deodand In old English law an object which has been the immediate cause of death would be forfeited to the Crown.

Fee farm rent Tenure by fee simple at a fixed rent without services.

Gaile or quarter money County rates paid quarterly through the parish officers.

Glebe Land granted to an incumbent as part of his benefice or income.

Glyster An enema.

Heraldic terms Dexter – right
Or – Gold
Sinister – Left
Argent (arg) – Silver
Azure – Blue
Fretty – Interlaced
Gules – Red
Annulet – a little circle denoting the fifth son

Sable – Black
Vert – green

Heriot   After the death of a tenant the lord of the manor had the right to claim as heriot the best beast belonging to the deceased and sometimes the parish priest had the right to the second best animal.

Hundred   An ancient division of a county in England.

Imprimis, imp   In the first place.

King's Evil   The custom of touching by the king for the cure of scrofula was very popular in Charles II's time. Scrofula was a tuberculosis of the lymph nodes in the neck. Charles used a gold medalet or touchpiece for the ceremony. To prevent abuse of the system numbers were limited and those who were admitted had to provide a certificate from their parish priest and churchwardens. A record had to be kept of this in the parish books.

Leasow(e)   A pasture or meadow.

Lewnes (leawne)   A levy or rate especially in Shropshire and neighbouring counties.

Marle pit   A pit where marl or calcareous clay was dug for use as fertiliser.

Messuage   A dwelling with its adjoining offices and lands.

Money
l or li   £1

	(the 'l' comes from the Latin *libra* a pound, hence we get the '£' sign)
S or s	Shilling (from the Latin *solidus*) equivalent of 12 old pennies, or 5 new pence.
D or d	An old penny (from the Latin *denarius*)
Overseers of the Poor	Two, three or four of these were to be nominated each year and were to be substantial householders in the parish. They had the duty of maintaining and setting to work the poor in the parish with funds provided by local taxation.
Park pale	The enclosed park.
Pass	A settlement certificate given by a parish to a poor person leaving it, guaranteeing that they would be received back again if they proved chargeable.
Pole	Thirty and a quarter square yards.
Quitrent	A rent payable by a freeholder to his lord that released him from liability to perform duties to that lord.
Recusants	Roman Catholics who refused to attend the parish church.
Rood	Quarter of an acre, or 0.10117 hectares.
Serjeant	In full it is Serjeant-at-law; formerly a high-ranking barrister.
Tenement	A dwelling used by one family.

Tithe (tythe)   A tenth of the produce of the land or stock was taken as a tax for church purposes. Any levy or fee of one tenth.

Vagrants   Vagrants were classified by the 1743 Act into three groups - 'idle and disorderly persons', 'rogues and vagabonds' and 'incorrigible rogues'. The constable of each area would take a vagrant to the boundary of the next area and so the vagrant would be returned by the quickest route to his place of settlement.

Vermin   In 1532 an act ordered a rate of 2d. to be paid for every 12 crows, or rooks or choughs that were caught. Later this included sparrows' heads or eggs and fox heads.

Workhouse   In 1722 overseers and churchwardens were able to set up workhouses for those poor who were unable to find work. Those who refused to go into a workhouse would no longer be entitled to any relief.

The churchwardens' chest of Tong - "This Chest, with its three locks to prevent Vicar or Churchwardens opening it unless all three were present and agreed" – showing the three locks; one for the vicar and one for each churchwarden.

And in the accounts for 1630 are the following entries:-

Paid for the chest lidde	*xxd*
Given to the Joyner for plaininge it	*vid*
For three lockes three hinges with nayles	
and setting on for a coffer	*vs*

"Into this chest were put all the things belonging to the church."

Notes on the History of Tong from the Parish Books.

Volume 2

The third notebook

of

John Ernest Auden

Vicar of Tong, 1896 - 1913

There are in the Church chest at Tong the Registers dating from May 19th. 1629, a book containing the churchwardens' accounts 1630-1675, and also certain other entries up to 1682; another containing accounts from 1810 to the present time, several bundles of papers relating to bonds with the parish, apprenticeship of children, receipts for briefs etc.; and two M.S. notebooks compiled by the Rev. R. G. Lawrance, Vicar of Tong 1870-75. The following notes consist in the main of extracts from these telling in their own words, as far as possible, the history of the parish.

With regard to the book of the **Churchwardens' accounts** the following is written on the first page.

"This volume, containing the Churchwardens' accounts from

1630-1680, various entries of Births, Burials etc., and other interesting matter connected with the Parish of Tong, Salop, was placed in a torn and dilapidated state (as found by him) by Mr. Harding at the service of Stephen Tucker[1], when collecting materials for his history of Tong in 1860. At whose cost and instance it was bound and preserved from further decay, not only to mark the importance he set upon its proper keeping, but as a small acknowledgement of 'the courtesy and assistance accorded to him in his investigations by Mr. Harding'."

In the year 1630 Tong Castle was owned by Sir Thomas Harries, Bart., who had bought it from Sir Edward Stanley in 1603. Sir Thomas, after having achieved fame as a lawyer, was created a Baronet in 1622/3. His wife was Ellinor, daughter of Roger Gifford, M.D., physician to Queen Elizabeth and President of the Royal College of Physicians, who died 1597.

The whole of the parish, however, did not belong to him for the site of the College still belonged to a descendant of James Wooleitch who bought it at the Dissolution of Religious Houses; a tenement and land at Tong Norton belonged to the Marion family then and till 1875; the Duncalfs owned property at Tong; Ruckley Grange belonged to Richard Vernon; the land between Lizard Grange and Burlington to Sir Richard Levison; Hubbal Grange to the Giffards, as did also land at Neachley Brook[2] besides small freeholders owning land at Norton.

The Churchwardens in 1630 were Roger Austen of Ruckley Grange and Thomas Halfpenny. They seem to have found the parish ill provided with books or a place to keep them in[3], and

---

[1] afterwards Rougecroix Pursuivant at Arms (note in handwriting of Rev. R.G. Lawrance)

[2] In 1739 The Fitzherberts owned several parcels of land in Tong Parish, part of that formerly belonging to Neachley, the Grange Farm of White Ladies. Some of this was not united to the Tong Estate until 1855.

[3] Thomas Cromwell's injunction came into operation Sept. 29, 1538.
On Sept. 5 he, having recently been appointed Vicar General, issued a series of injunctions, including this one:-

the former at once set about getting what was necessary; for the Churchwardens' book begins thus:

"This booke was bestowed by Roger Austen of Ruckley Grandge, one of the Churchewardens for the Towne and P'she of Tonge in Com. Salop, for the use of the Churchewardens for the keepinge of theire Accompts of the Churche hereafter. In the Syxte yeare of the Raigne of our Sovraigne Lorde Charles now kynge of Englande. Anno Dm. 1630."

And in his accounts for **1630** are the following entries:-

Paid for a chest lidde	xx d.
Given to the Joyner for plaininge it	vi d.
For three lockes three hinges with nayles and setting on for a coffer	v s.
Paid for a register booke of parchment, being twelve skins made into sixe and thirtie leaves	vii s.
For two Journeys to Bridgenorth for a regester booke in kausinge it to be made and fetchinge it spent	xii d.

Into this chest were put all the goods belonging then to the Church, for Mr. Austen writes:-
Memorandum: that these thinges hereafter nominated are left in a chest newlye repaired by Roger Austen one of the Churchwardens of the P'ishe of Tonge 1630.

---

*That you and every parson, vicare or curate shall for every churche kepe **one boke or registere** wherein ye shall write the day and yere of every weddyng, christenying and buryeng made within your parishe for your tyme, and so for every man suceedyng you likewise. And shall insert every persons name that shall be so weddid, christened or buried. (State Papers).*
Then followed directions for the provision by the parish of **"one sure coffer with two locks and keys,"** in which to keep the book. Entries were to be made every Sunday, in the presence of at least one warden, of all the weddings, etc., made the whole week before.
The 70th. Canon of 1603 enjoined that the Registers be kept in a **"sure coffer with three locks and keys"**.

Imp: one Bible, one Comunion booke, two bookes of homilies, one booke of Canons, a booke called a defence of the Apologie of the Church of England, The Paraphrase of Erasmus[4], a regester booke.
Item: one Comunion Cuppe with a cover[5], a cloth of silke and one of diaper for the Comunion table.
Item: fower towels.
Item: a pulpett cloth of blacke, and a cloth of blacke to cover the Bere at anye Buriall.
Item: a surplus.

This chest, with its three locks to prevent Vicar or Churchwardens opening it unless all three were present and agreed, is still in the vestry, and the Register purchased by Roger Austen is the earliest extant. For, though William Mytton (died 3 Sept. 1746) quotes in his M.S. extracts from the Shropshire Registers "a Roll beginning in 1588 imperfect," which he found at Tong, it has

---

[4] By a proclamation of **1541 every parish was ordered to "buy and provide Bibles** of the largest and greatest volume, and cause the same to be set and fixed in the Parish Church." The price of the Bible unbound was settled at 10s. - 'i.e. about £6. 10s. 0d. of our money' [*as Auden writes about 1900*] or 12s. "Well and sufficiently bound, trimmed and clasped." This was the Great Bible.
The **"English Order of Communion" appeared in 1548.** It was not a full Communion Office, but an English form for the people, grafted on to the Latin Office for the Mass.
The **First Book of Homilies was printed in 1547**, and is ascribed to Cranmer, Ridley, Latimer, Bonnor and the latter's chaplain. The Second Book was published in 1563 and was mainly the work of Jewel.
The **Constitutions and Canons Ecclesiastical** were published in 1604, and "the Book of the said Canons was ordered to be provided at the charge of the Parish".
The **Paraphrase of Erasmus** was in 1547 ordered to be placed beside the Gospels in some convenient place in every church that the parishioners might read it.
Bishop Jewel's **"Defence of the Apologie of the Churche of Englande,** conteininge an Answeare to a certaine Booke lately set forth by Mr. Hardinge," was also ordered to be kept in churches.
[5] On June 2, 1553 Tong possessed a **chalice of copper** partially gilt, all that was left by the King's Commissioners of the goods which no doubt had once belonged to the church, the gifts of pious benefactors.
Fulke Eyton e.g. by his will dated 1454 bequeathed to the Warden and Priests of the College of Tong his **"best Basin and Eure of Silver,"** and **"to the Chapell of our Lady of Tong his Chalice and his blew vestiment of damaske of his armes."** William Fitzherbert in 1451 bequeathed "a gown for making vestments." Before 1855 there were at Tong Castle "two mediaeval thuribles which were said to have been formerly used in Tong church" and bought at the sale of the Duke of Kingston's property in 1764. (H. F. J. Vaughan in S.A.S.T. vol. 2, (1879).)

now disappeared, and the first existing register is headed "The regester for the p'ish of Tong beginninge the 19th. May ano. Domin. 1629." The vicar of Tong at the time was the Rev. George Meeson described in an Elizabethan clergy list of 1602 as "no preacher, no degree."(i.e. held no degree and was not licensed by his Bishop to preach.)[6] However he wrote a good clear hand as may be seen from his signature.

In the first two years there are few entries worth quoting, but the following may be taken as samples.

1629. ffoulke the sonne of George Meeson was buried the vi[th] day of June.
ffrancis the daughter of Richard Dippere als. Marrion and Elizabeth his wyfe was buried the XXIIIrd. day of December.
(1590 June 1. Frauncis Marrian als Dippard bap.- Brewood Register - so the alias is of long standing).

1630 Thomas the sonne of Thomas Peanton[7] and Margaret his wife was baptized the 30th day of August.

---

[6] S. A. S. T. 2nd series Vol 5.

[7] The will of John Peynton of Tong Norton, dated 30 March 1579, proved 1582, is at Lichfield. After a religious exordium the testator desires his "bodye to be buried in the churchyard of Tonge" and adds: Item: I give and bequeath to John Peinton, my youngest son, my best washinge basyn and my best chaffinge dyshe, yf ye said John dye without children then I will that ye sayde basyn and chaffinge dyshe shall remayne unto John Peynton ye sonne of Raphe Peynton. Item I gyve to ye sayde John my sonne one t'winter bullock. Item: I gyve to John Peynton the sonne of Raphe two sheepe to be delyvered unto him by ye sayde John my sonne. Item: I gyve and bequeath to Alice Peynton my yongest daughter one cowe which nowe ys at my howse knowen and called by ye name "Lovelye" .Item: I give and bequeath to Agnes Peynton, my third daughter, one cowe to be delyvered unto her by the direction of Elizabeth my wyfe. (etc etc disposing of goods and cattle). Residue to Elizabeth my wyfe, (after debts payde) to be used at her discretion with the assent and consent of my two eldest sonnes for the bryinging up of my children etc. after Elizabeth my wyfe's diceas to be divided among my children. I do ordain and make Elizabeth my wyffe and Raphe Peynton my eldest sonne exors.

In the presence of Wm. Rudge curate of Tonge, and of Thomas Peynton curate of Norton cum aliis inventory indifferently prysed and valued by these indifferent and honest men To witt
    Thomas Clarke of Liziard Grange
    Robert Barbur of the p'ish of Norton
    John Walker of Tonge
Imprimis iiij oxen of which one due unto the Lord for an heriot valued at vij li.
Sum total xl li. iijs. iiijd.
Proved 9th August 1582.

Thomas Richards and Sara Hill were maried by speciall lycence the 2nd day of September.

ffrancis the daughter of William Peripoynt and Elizabeth (his) wyfe was borne the 1st daye of September 1630 and baptized the 13th daye of October.

Anne the daughter of Thomas Duncaulfe and Joan his wife was baptized the 30th day of Januarie.

The entries in the churchwardens accounts are far more interesting and show what energetic men held the office in 1630. (It may however be said in preface that of the two wardens, one was originally chosen to represent the township of Tong, and the other the township of Tong Norton, and that they almost always kept separate accounts, which are entered on separate pages).[8] The following are some extracts from their entries.

The Accounts of Roger Austen one of the churchwardens for the p'ishe of Tonge Ano Dm:1630

For a booke of Articles and one oather	ii s
For a case of Buccoram[9] for the surpluse	x d
Given to a strange preacher	ii s
Paid to William Eadmons for mason's work about the church for sixe dayes	vi s
For his man sixe dayes	iiii s
Paid to him and his man for two dayes pointinge the steeple	iiii s
Laide downe towardes dischardinge the glasier of Shifnall for repayring the church windowes	viii s
Paide for castinge a bell brasse and putting it in and a plate	iiii s
For crampes and pins for the steeple	v d
For sixe poundes and a halfe of soyder and mending the leades	ix s

---

[8] Tong Norton (i.e. Tong North town) had a separate history from Tong as early as 1167 when each was fined for an offence against the Forest laws. (Griffith's History of Tong, p.144). It lies due north from Tong village.

[9] Buccoram i.e. Buckram, coarse linen cloth, stiffened with glue or gum: Latin brandium.

For mending the dore and the hinges for the leades	vi d
For a kay and mendinge the locke for the vestrie house dore	i s
Paid for repayringe a reale of pales that noe man would owne to William Wood	iii d
Given unto a poore man of Pattingham which had losse by fire & had a certificate to gather in his neighoods churches	xii d
Paid for gaile money & maymed souldiers for one quarter[10]	iiis xid
Paid for ringinge on the kinges holye day [11]	iis

---

[10] By an act passed by Eliz. (1598) the relief of maimed soldiers & sailors was placed on the parochial assessment.

[11] The following copy of the original proclamation for the observance of the 5th of November is still preserved in M.S. amongst the parish papers in the church chest.

Anno 3 Jacobi Regis

An Act for a publique thanksgiving to Almighty God every yeare on the 5th of November. Forasmuch as Almighty G. hath in all ages shewed his power and mercy in the miraculous and gracious deliverance of his church & in ye p'tection of Religious Kinges & states & that noe nation of ye earth hath bin blest with greater benefitts than this kingdome now enioyeth, having ye true & free p'session of ye Gospell under our most Soveraigne Lord King James - the most great, learned and religious kinge that ever reigned therein,- wicht with a most hopefull and plentifull progenie p'ceeding out of his royall loynes, promising continuance of this happinesse & p'fession to all posterity: the wch many malignant and divilish papists Jesuists and Seminary Priests much envyinge and fearing conspired most horribly, when the king's most excellent maiesty, the Queene, the Prince and all the Lords spirituall and temporall and commons should have bin assembled in the Upper House of Parliament upon ye fifth day of November in ye yeare of our Lord 1605 suddenly to have blowne up the said whole house with gunpowder an invention soe inhumane barbarous and cruell as the like was never before heard of and was (as some of the principall conspirators thereof confessed) purposely devised and concluded to be done in ye said house that whereas sundry necessary and religious lawes for the p'servation of ye church and state were made, which they falsely and slanderously tearme cruell lawes enacted against them and their religion, both place and persons should be all destroyed and blowne up at once, which would have turned to the utter ruine of this whole kingdome; had it not pleased Almighty God by inspiring the king's most excellent maiestie with a divine Spirit to interpret some darke phrases of a letter shewed to his maiestie above and beyonde all ordinary construction, thereby myraculously discovering this hidden treason not many hours before ye appointed time for ye execution thereof. Therefore the king's most excellent maiesty, the Lords spirituall and temporall and all his maiestie's most faithfull and loving subjects doe most iustly acknowledge this greate and infinit blessinge to have p'ceded mearely from God's greate mercie, & to his most holy name doe ascribe all honor glory and praise.

And to the end this unfaigned thankfullnesse may never be forgotten but be had in a perpetuall remembrance that all ages to come may yielde praise to his divine maiesty for the same, and have in memory this ioyfull day of deliverance. Be it so enacted by the king's most excellent maiestie the Lords Spirituall and temporall and the commons in this p'sent parliament assembled and by the authority of ye same that all and singular ministers in every Cathedrall and P'sh

Received of Humfrey Yearle for the breakinge
uppe of the church floore for the burienge of
Mrs Frauncis Giffordes grave   iiis iiiid

Brewood Register

*1612-3 Feb 12. Frauncis, d. of John Gifford of the Whyte Ladies, bap.
(Brewood Register)*

*1613-4 Jan 29. Dorothy, d. of John Gyfford of White Ladies, Esquire,
bap. (Brewood Register)*

1624 Dec 21. Margaret Gifford of Whit Ladies, bur. (Brewood Register)

1625 July 13. Mistress Frances Gifford of White Ladies bur. (Brewood Register)

The Accounts of Thomas Halfpenye one of the churchwardens of the p'ishe of Tonge Ano. Dmi 1630.

Paide for wyne for a communion at Whitsontide	xii d
Paide for halfe a strike of heaire	ii d
Paid for a tugge for the greate Bell	ii d
Paid for three pintes of winne for a Communion	xii d
Paid for the mendinge of the church walls	iiii s
Paid to Humfrey Duncalfe for the killinge of a foxe in the p'ishe	xii d

---

church or other usuall place for common praier within this Realme of England and dominions of
ye same shall allwaies upon ye fifth day of Nov say morning prayer and give unto Almighty G.
thanks for this most happy deliverance & that all and every p'son and p'sons inhabiting within
this Realme of England and the Dominons of ye same shall allwaies upon that day diligently and
faithfully resort to ye Psh church or chappell accustomed or to some usual church or chapel
where ye said morning praier, preaching or other service of G. shall be used and then and there
to abide orderly & soberly during the time that the said praiers & p'reaching or other service of G
there to be used and ministered ... all & every p'son may be put in minde of this duty and be ye
better p'pared to the said holy service be it enacted by authority aforesaid that every minister
shall give warning to his p'shners (-----) in ye church at Morning Praier the Sunday before every
such 5 day of November for ye due observation of ye saide daie and that after morning praier
and p'ching upon ye said 5 day of November they reade distinctly and plainely this p'sent Act.
God save ye Kinge.

In the registers of the next year 1631, are scarcely any entries worth transcribing.

George Salter and Elizabeth Bennet were married the 7th of July.

Ellinor the daughter of William Peripoynt Esquier and Elizabeth his wyfe bapt. 4th of September.

John the sonne of John Baddeley and Elizabeth his wyfe was bapt the 2nd of March.

In the account of Thomas Lateward are the following

Given to a souldier	iiii d
Payd for a boxe to gather for the poore	iii d
For hanging a dore for the porch	iii s viiid
For mending the clocke	is vi d

The accounts of his fellow warden are not preserved, while in **1632** we have again only

Thomas Scott's accounts

Lead out at Bridgnorth a monthly sitting	xiiii d
Payd to Thomas Twigg[12] for the porch dore	vii s

In the Register we find in **1632**

Margreat the daughter of William Peripoynt Esquire and Elizabeth his wyfe bapt. 22nd Oct.

For the years **1633 and 1634** we have no churchwarden's accounts and but few interesting entries in the registers.

1633 Mr. George Broune & Mrs. Anne Scrimshawe were married by speaciall lycence the 16th Dec.

1634 Mrs. Dorothy Giffard was buried the 10th of July.

Robert the sonn of William Peripoynt Esquire and Elizabeth his wyfe was borne & bapt the 27th Sept.

1634 Indenture between Lady Harris & John Cooke.

Thomas Woulleston was buried the last day of Jannuarie.

---

[12] 1653 Nov 4. Thomas Twigg of Donington, carpenter & householder buried (Donington Register)

On the west tie-beam in Donington Ch. is carved Thomas Twigg, carpenter,1635.

This Mrs. Dorothy Gifford was[13] the wife of John Gifford the builder of Boscobel House, whose reason for giving it this name is to be found in Hughes Boscobel Tracts (ed 1837) p. 195. John Gifford was the son of the widow of William Skeffington of White Ladies by her third husband.

In "the accounts made by George Salter and Thomas Clarke churchwardens for the parrish of Tonge in the yeares of our Lord God 1635 and 1636" we find no mention of the bell now in the steeple bearing the inscription "Gloria in excelsis Deo 1636" unless the bell ropes refer to it. Probably it was a free gift and all the expenses were paid by the donor. On May 25 1553 there were "three bellys remainyng wythin the steeple of Tonnge", of which the Big Bell is now probably the only survivor, the latter being given in 1518 and twice recast since. The dates on the other bells in order of time are 1593; 1605; 1623; 1636; 1719; 1810; (this last in place of a much older one which was sold that year).

	£	s	d
Laid out at the Archbishop's visitation at Shrewsbury for ffees		4	10
Paid for 2 bellropes the 27th of June		6	0
Paid for wier for the clocke			4
Paid the joyner for the frame aboute the communion table	1 li	4	0
Paid for mates to knelle at the communion			6
Paid Thomas Holmes towards the building of Bes Greenes house		12	0
Paid the Clarkes bill the first year		2	0
Paid at my Lord Bishopes visitation held at Newporte the first of June 1636 for fees there		4	10
Paid for glasing the church windowes		5	0

---

[13] [Auden adds a note in pencil saying 'apparently not'.]

Boscobel House built by John Gifford about 1630 to shelter Roman Catholics.

Paid for 2 bookes for the faste [14]	2	0
Paid Whitmore for hanging the greate bell anew	15	4
Paid for a rope for the greate bell	4	6
Paid Twigge his bill for mending the church-yarde gate	18	2
Paid for fatching the bordes downe	1	6
Paid for hillinge three graves and other work about the church	3	0
Receaved for 3 graves	10	0

Receaved for a peese of mettle which was broken of the greate bell	1	12	8

The Archbishop of Canterbury in 1636 was William Laud, appointed in 1633 and executed in 1645. According to the S.A.S.T. I.X., (1886) p179, the Archbishop did not come himself (he had been there in Aug. 1632), but sent his Vicar-general, Sir Nathaniel Brent, to enquire into church matters. The Bishop of Lichfield in 1636 was Robert Wright who, after having been chaplain to Queen Elizabeth and James I and Bishop of Bristol, was appointed to Lichfield in 1632 and died in 1643 after having suffered 18 months imprisonment in the Tower for his loyalty. The churchwardens had enough visitations in these two years for their Archdeacon held his at Newport on Oct 15; May 27; Oct 7 1636; and May 3 1637; at all 6 they had to pay their usual fees.

The work done in connection with the communion table was owing to injunctions given by the Archbishop in this year, that **all altars should be "rayled in" as a protection against dogs**, which at that time were not infrequently allowed in churches, a "hall dog pew" for the squires' dogs being provided in some edifices.

---

[14] A terrible outbreak of the plague occurred in 1636. On October 18th a form of prayer and fasting on Wednesdays during the continuance of the visitation was issued. One of the charges against Archbishop Laud was for certain alterations he made in the book for the fast of this year. (The Guardian Feb 14. 1900 p 239).

Bes Greene must have been one of the parish poor, she did not however long enjoy her new house, for her burial is entered on March 31st 1638.

The entries concerning **the Big Bell,** and especially the selling of a piece broken off it, shew that the inscription "Perduellionum rabie fractam" put on at its recasting in 1720, is bad history. For the rabies perduellionum did not burst forth till 1642, ista tamen campana certe fracta erat anno Dom. 1636[15].

In the register for **1635** we find
Dame Ellinor Harres was buried the 9th of April.
Hugh Ranfford beinge sleane by unfortunate accedent was buried the 10th of April.

John Halfpenny was buried the 2nd of May.

And for the various entries from **May 3 1636 to Feb 16 1637-8**, we have the original entries made in the churchwardens account book, which was used for that time as a **day book**, and from it copied into the Register at the time the copy was made ready for presentation at the Visitation. The entries of Burials are much fuller than in the Register as will be seen from the following, for all that comes after the date is wanting in the Register.

John Wheeler was buried the 5th of May and lyeth three yards southe est ffrom the East Corner of the goulden Chapple.

Anne the wyffe of Thomas Scott was buried the 28th of June her head lyinge three footes ffrom the west Corner of the goulden Chapple.

Mrs. Margreat Harres buried the 17th of August close adioyning to Mr. ffrancis Harres on the southe syde.

Margere the wyffe of Houmfry Smyth was buried the 2nd of December, and lyeth 5 yards from the crosse eastwards.

---

[15] [*Perduellionum rabie fractam* - broken in the madness of the Civil war. *ista tamen campana certe fracta erat anno Dom. 1636* - Indeed that bell was certainly broken in the year of our Lord 1636.]

Elizabeth the daughter of George Salter and Elizabeth his wyffe was buried the 4th of January 1636 and lyeth betwixt Mr. Bennets seat and Jeffery Weightwicks against the middle of them both.

Mr. Thomas Lakwood was buried the 14th day of Januarie and lyeth betwixt his owne seat and Vernons toume p't of him in his owne seate.

Anne the daughter of John Cartwright was buried the 20th of January and lyeth on the derect ligne betwixt the middle of the Crosse and the yew tree towards harrisons nyne yards distance from the Crosse where his granffather and granmother lye.

Elizabeth the wyffe of Mr. Georg Salter was buried the fforth day of ffebruarie and lyeth on the north side vere nere adioyning to her chylde being betwixt her father Mr. Bennets seat and the north end of Jeffrery Weightwicks pew.

Renald Hampton was buried the 25th of ffebruarie and lyeth eight yards from the east end of the porch wickett in the derect line to the Colleidg.

"Dame Ellinor Harres" was the widow of Sir Thomas Harres,[16]

[16] Thomas Harris was the eldest son of John Harries esq. of Cruckton, was bap at Pontesbury 23rd Jan 1549 and admitted of Shrewsbury School in 1565; he became a Serjeant in 1589; purchased Tong Castle; was created a baronet in 1624, died soon after (O & B History of Shrewsbury I p379). Put up as MP for Shrewsbury 1584 Nov 23, voting Thomas Owyne 366; Robert Barker 299, Tho Harris 176. MP 1586 Oct 29 to 1589 Feb 4. (O & B. I. 550.)
John Harris of Cruckton in the manor of Ford had 4 sons; Sir Thomas of Tong Castle, Rowland of Ludlow; Arthur of Prescot and Richard who succeeded to the estate of Cruckton, as the youngest son according to the custom of Borough English in the manor of Ford.
Francis Harris (?) only son of Sir Thomas Harris of Tong, entered Merton Coll. Oxon.
Visitation of Shrop. 1623

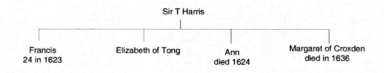

The king gave licence to Sir Edward Stanley to alienate the manor of Tong, Salop to Thomas Harris, serjeant at law, afterwards knight and baronet: which Harris had issue one son and two daughters. The son died in his youth; the eldest daughter Anne married John Wylde of Droit-

the late owner of Tong Castle estate, who died in 1628. She was the daughter of Roger Gifford of Lindon, physician to Queen Elizabeth, and was also **a most munificent benefactor to Tong** as will be seen from the list of her gifts in the ch'wardens' book.

"A note of the ornaments and goodes apptayning to this one Church of Tonge hereafter severally named; lyinge most part of them in a chest repayred by Roger Austans Churchwarden in anno, dom. 1630. Memorandum: that these ornaments first nominated are the free guift of the honourable Dame Ellinor Harres Lady to Sir Thomas Harres Barronett.

---

wich, co Worcester, and died 6 May 1624 in 16th year; Elizabeth the other daughter married William Pierrepoint of Thoresby, co Notts, by whom she had five sons. (Originalia 6&7 James I, 1st 9(1607-9).

Arms granted to Harries of Tong Castle in July 1604, Crest a hawk <u>arg</u>, beaked and belled <u>or</u>, preying on a pheasant of the first.

Sir Thomas Harries was the eldest son of John Harries of Cruckton. He was born January1549-50; bap. at Pontesbury 23 Jan; entered Shrewsbury School in 1565; afterwards a student of the Middle Temple. Was made a serjeant at law in 1589, was knighted in 1603 and made a baronet April 12 1623, then of Tong Castle. "died soon after" (O. & B. I .379). In 1584 he was MP for Callington Cornwall; in 1586 for Shrewsbury and 1589 for Portsmouth; in 1592 and 1597 for Bossiney in Cornwall, in 1601 for Truro. In 1603 he purchased Tong Castle from Sir Edward Stanley and died circa 1628.

His sister Margaret married Thomas Ottley of Pitchford. She was born in 1576 and was buried at Pitchford in 1642. She was the mother of Sir Francis b. 1601, High Sheriff 1645, and had other sons and 5 daughters.
Sir Thos Harrys serjeant at law bought the property of the dissolved abbey of Croxden, co Stafford from Godfrey Foljambe, to whose father Geoffrey it had been granted at the Dissolution.
Sir T.H.'s only son died soon after the purchase. He passed this and Tong Castle in Shropshire to William Pierpoint Esq, younger son of the Earl of Kingston who married the serjeant's daughter (Eardeswick Harwoods p 504).
Croxden one of the Foljambs had, and died a beggar in a barn after he had sold it to Serjeant Harris, who had a hopeful son, who died soon after the purchase, by which it came into a strange family. (Simon Degge - 20 Feb 1669).

"Imp a comunion cup of Goulde & christall; a yewer and plate of sil-ver, a cloth for the communion table of diaper; the Pulpitt; a clothe and cushion of velvet workt with silver for the Pulpitt; a Pulpitt clothe of black onely for funerrall sarmonts. A black clothe to cover the biere at all burialls".
"These underwritten p'vyded att the charge of the p'yshe".

Then follows a repetition of the articles enumerated above by Roger Austen.

Lady Harries also gave £100 to the parish for apprenticing poor children.

The "cup of goulde and christall" has been pronounced by Mr. St. John Hope to be "a unique German drinking vessel of the time of Henry VIII;"
 the "ewer" (hallmark 1606) is a silver round bellied flagon with dragon headed spout, standing 12½ inches high[17]; the "plate of silver" is a small paten (hallmark 1627-8, maker's initials A.I.) with the shield of the Harris family (barry of 7 erm and az over all 3 annulets or. two and one);
"the cloth for the Pulpit", now preserved in a glass case in the vestry bears 4 scrolls, 2 of "cor unum, via una"[18]; and 2 of "use bien tempo."
The black cloth for pulpit and bier have disappeared.
The pulpit bears the inscription "Ex ano. Dom. Harries 1629".

---

[17] [In 2004 this ewer was in the Victoria and Albert Museum, London.]
[18] Cor unum, via una [one heart, one way] is the motto of the Marquis of Exeter. The connection may be a friendship between Roger Gifford, physician to Queen Elizabeth and his daughter Lady Harries and the great Cecil, Lord Burleigh, the Queen's High Treasurer.

The Tong Cup is now securely exhibited in Lichfield Cathedral.

The following for **1637** are again taken from the churchwarden's book:

Joane the wyfe of John Sutton was buried the 10th of May and lyeth 2 yards distant ffrom the crosse betwixt it and the castle churchyard gate.

John the sonne of Andrew Powell was buried the 18th day of May and was lead upon the banke before the church dore upon the left hand the way going ffromward the church.

Elizabeth the daughter of Harrey Wetwicke was buried the 30th day of May and lyeth within a quarter of a yard of the north est corner of the Crosse.

Thomas Baddeley of Tong & Mary fforster of Davenport parochia Asbury Comit. Chester, were married the 29th of May.

Alice Newman was buried the 11th of June and lyeth seaven yards distant ffrom the crosse west ward.

Margere Cartleich widdow was buried the 28th of June and lyeth in the middest way betwixt the crosse and the colledg.

Henry the sonne of the right hon. William Perrepoint Esq.[19] and Elizabeth his wife was bap. the 15th of August.

Mary the wyffe of Morris Yeavans was buried the 28th of November and is buried directly against the south dore.

William Carelesse sonne of ffraunce Carelesse and Grace his wife was bur. the 9th of December.

This Francis Careless was a nephew of the famous **Colonel William Careless**, who assisted Charles II to escape after Worcester in Sept. 1651. According to the S.A.S.T., 2nd series vol 1. p.85, in 1654, William Careless, son of William Careless, Governor of Tong Castle, was admitted to the Jesuits College at Rome; (the Dict.of Nat. Biog., & the pedigree in Hughes' Boscobel speak of a son named William, though Alan Fea does not), The following pedigree is from the "Flight of the King" p.307 with the exception of the names in ( ).

---

[19] The Duke of Kingston's family name is variously spelt, we have Pierrepont, Pierrepoint and Pierpont. The D.N.B. has Pierrepont, and we may take it this is correct.

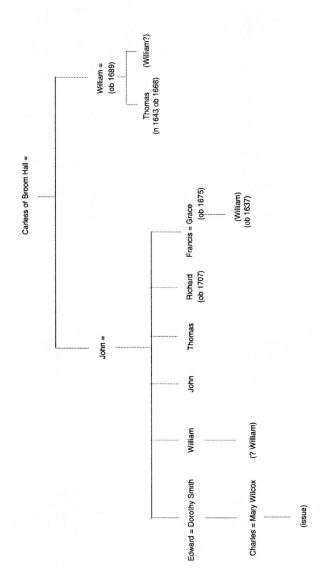

It is probable that the date 1654 only refers to the admission to the college, and not to the period of governorship, and that it was the more famous William and not his nephew, who was governor of Tong Castle at the time the younger William Careless was born. "This Colonel William Carlis was born at Bromhall in Staffordshire, within two miles of Boscobel, of good parentage, was a person of approved valour, and engaged all along in the first war for King Charles I[20] so he may have been for a short time governor of Tong Castle when the Royalists held it, since in 1654 Tong Castle was the residence of William Pierrepoint, a strong Parliamentarian and friend of Oliver Cromwell[21].

From the Accompte of Thomas Scott Churchwarden in Anno Dni 1637 we get

Paid the ringers at Joane Sutton's buriall	2	0
To Mr. Meeson and the Clarke		1
To Blakemores wife being sicke		6
To those that watched with her		6
To the ringers at her buriall	2	0
To Mr. Meeson		4
For a sheet for Blakemores wife[22]	2	0
To Mr. Davies when he viewed the church	2	6
To Roger Yearsly for whipping doggs out of the church	1	0

[20] Hughes' Boscobel Tracts p.248.

[21] 1689, May 28th, *burried Cornall William Carelesse of Bromhall. (Brewood Register)*
William Carless entered English Coll. at Rome 1654. Afterwards became S.J. and died Jan. 26, 1679. (H. Foley, Records of English Province S.J. Vol VI 391) An interesting paper by him, Foley vol.1 p 180,181)
William Careless jun. at age of 20 joined Chas. at Worcester in 1657. Was about 24 when admitted to coll.
William Pendrill, alias Birch, and William Pendrill, alias Howe entered Society of Jesus.
Richard Pendrill entered 1702, aged 21, to minor orders 1705.
William Carlos of Stafford, son of Colonel William Carlisse died 19th May, 1688 in the 25th year of his age, and was buried at Fulham, in which church is a monument with inscription and verses. Was apparently born 1664.

[22] It was customary in byegone times to bury without coffins but merely in a winding sheet. (see Andrew's Old Church Life pp 98-116.) Coffins indeed were rarely used until the year 1660 except in the cases of the rich and people of affluence. cf. St. Michael's, Lichfield; "1632, Dec.1. Andrew the sonne of William Burnes buried with a coffin".

To the Joyner for making Mr. Meesons pue[23]		6	0
To Thomas Twigge the carpenter for his worke at the church	8	3	10

Received of Alice Emery for a wastcoat & some ould things of Blakemores wifes		3	0
Received for lead Ashes	1	6	0

In Thomas Holmes accompte are

Given to the peticon of a poore minister being in Yorke gaole 27th June			6
Paid to the plummer	19	9	0

The total expenses of the two churchwardens for 1637 came to £46.15s.4d. - a very large sum for those days; the re-leading of the roof being the chief item.

In 1638 (during which year the Hon. William Pierrepont of Tong was High Sheriff of Shropshire) there are no entries worth copying from the Register, but the accounts of Morris Evans contain interesting notice of perquisites of a bishop's retinue in those days.

Paid to my lord Bishups officers at Weston Hall	2	6
To my lord Bishups macebearer & coachman	2	0
To my lord Bishups ffooteman		6
For beare for the ringers when my lord Bishup came to Tonge		6
My charges at Shrewsbury being called against recusants	2	0

---

[23]Vicar's pew in North Chapel. See terrier of 1759.

Evans also served in 1639, as also did Thomas Earle, his fellow warden, who left both years' accounts together. In the former's expenditure is

Given to a poore minister at the request of Mr.
Meeson   6

In the accounts of Thomas Earle for 1638 and 39 we find

Paid for three thraves of straw and drawing	3	6
Paid for thetching Dunkies howse	1	0
To a poore man that went to Ireland by passe		6
To a poore minister that came from Ireland		4
Paid for iron and workmanship for the greate bell & Claper	5	0
Paid for mending the bell	2	6
Charges for myselfe & horse at Shrewsbury against recusants	1	10
Paid for a ridle to ridle lime withal		4
Paid for mending the clocke		6
Paid for a rope for the greate poise for the clocke	3	4
To the parriter for bringing the King's P'climation against the Scotts[24]		6

There are also entries of payments to Roger Yearslie, the dog whipper, and the "geole money" now appears as "Quarter money". The mention of Ireland occurs over and over again in the gifts to poor strangers, Tong being close to the great road between Holyhead and London. There would probably be many recusants, or Roman Catholics, who refused to attend the services which the law prescribed in the parish e.g. the Pendrills of Hubbal Grange.[25]

---

[24] Proclamation against the Scots. In 1637 Charles I attempted to impose upon the Church of Scotland a liturgy. In 1638 the Scots drew up a document called the Covenant, which was signed by all ranks of society, by which they pledged themselves to resist all changes in religion. In 1639 Charles collected an army and marched against them, but when the two forces came in sight of each other, negotiations were opened and a temporary peace concluded.

[25] In a list of recusants in Shropshire 1591-2 (S.A.S.T. pt. iii. series 3,vol 1,1909, p 412) are the names William Jervis of Tonge, Humfrey Foster gent of Tong Norton and Edward Chatterton alias Chilton, of Tong, yeoman, and Katherine his wife.

"At Christmas 1640 Mr. Barneffeild of Hampton gave to the poore of Tong p'ishe two shillings and six pence and it was distributed as followeth".

The list of recipients shews that 14 persons received 2d each and 2 persons 1d, but it must be remembered that money had about 6 times the purchasing power that it has now and that 2s. 6d. would be worth 15s.

In the Register for 1639 & 40 we find

1639 George Cooke, the sonne of John Cooke and Mary his wife was bap. the 8th of Aprill, George Meeson Clerke, George Salter gent, Mrs. Anne Scott of Cosford, sureties.

Ellenor the wife of George Meeson was buryed the 4th of Maie.

Mary the daughter of David Jones and Elenor his wife was bapt. the 12th of October.

1640 Roger Eardesley was buryed the 2nd of Maie.

William the sonne of William Pierrepont and Elizabeth his wife was buryed the 13th Nov.

In the Churchwarden Ralph Homes' accounts for 1640

Spent when I went to Shrewsbury before the King's Commissioners about recusants goods	2	10
Spent at a visitation at Drayton the 15th of October	2	6
At the request of Mr. Meeson given to a man that had losse by fier	1	0
Given to a man that brought a lantterne from abbots bromly that was given to the church by one Richard Whiston	1	0
At the request of Mr. Meeson given to an Irishman that had greate losse by fier		6
Paid the Clarke for ringing curffew & Day bell	5	0

In churchwarden John Cooke's

Paid for a booke for the fast upon the 8th day of July[26]	2	0
Paid John Cartwright for mending a tombe in the bell howse,[27] & paid for lime and beare to mend that tombe	1	4
Paid ffees at the visitation at Michellmas and for a prayer to be red in the church in time of danger	1	8
Given to a gentleman that preached in our church	2	6
Paid John Swinshead for mending Dunkies Chimmy & for nailes for the same chimmy	3	6
Paid for clamstaves & windings for the same chimmy		7
Paid for carring ston & for making the asler & dawbing of Dunkies Chimmy	3	4
Given to a man that brought the lanthorne that Richard Whiston gave to the church	1	0
Paid the Clarke for ringing curffew & daybell in p'te	5	0

Troublous times now seem to have fallen on Tong, the churchwardens elected in 1641 held office for six years, proba-bly owing to the unsettled state of everything during the civil war, this parish being the scene of many encounters between the rival parties. The vicar too who had been in charge of the church for many years died, and he seems to have been compelled, ow-ing to old age, to have an assistant, for the entries in the Register for 1641 are headed "p'me Guiliel: Southall: Rectr."

---

[26]In 1640 Archbishop Laud drew up a form for a solemn fast to be observed in England and Wales on July 8th, when the Scots were threatening to invade England. (The Guardian ut supra).
[27]It is hard to say what the "bell howse" was; we meet with the expression again in 1684; perhaps the space under the tower.

1641

Elenor the daughter of Hugh Cleton and Ann his wife (mendicating travellers) was bapt. Nov the 28th.

George Salter, gent: was buried March ye 12th.

From the former we see that 250 years ago there were such persons as tramps.

From the accounts of Edward Bishton in 1641, (the other churchwardens are not preserved),

Given the carter that fetched the stocke for the greate bell	1	0
Spent in beare at the same time		6
Paid to John Baddeley towards mending the greate bell	9	0
Paid for mending the greate bell rope		3
Paid Thomas Meare for ringing curfew & day bell	5	0
Spent at Shrewsbury when I went to bring in the bene volence & for Riting the names of those that gave the bene volence	2	0

Edward Bishton puts the accounts of 1642 & 43 together, and his entries for 1644, 1645 & 1646 are very few, though entered separately; John Poole on the other hand presents his accounts for 1642 to 1644 (inclusive) all together. Evidently there were no vestry meetings during these years.

The following are from Edward Bishton's
1642 and 1643

Paid John Cartwright for poynting the steeple & for laying grave stones & other worke about the church	9	0
Paid for wortte to make the morter to poynt the steeple[28]		8
Paid for crampes for the steeple	6	6

---

[28] In former days the mixing of lime with wort or ale was very usual; more especially in preparing the mortar for churches. It was said to make the joints as difficult to sunder as the solid stone. In the churchwardens accounts of St Mary's Church, Shrewsbury is the following entry "40 gallaunds of the best worte are charged at 6d the gallaund, and 3s for eggs."

1644

Paid Thomas Twigg for squarring & sawing of timber	5	6
Paid to the Cananere for the redeeming of the little bell	6	0

1645

Paid the sawyers for sawing of timber towards the repayring of the church	6	0
Paid for a rope for the little bell	1	6

1646

My charges to Shrewsbury to the comities	1	0
My charges to Bridgnorth being commanded thither before the Comities	1	0
Laid out for the Directory book & other ordinances to be read in the church which were given in church	1	0
Paid the joyner for worke about the church	14	9
Given to a preacher by consent of some of the neighbours	1	0

Among the entries of John Poole for the years 1642, 43, 44, 45 and 46 are

Paid for squaring and sawing of timber	6	0
Paid for lime to mend the church	5	6
Paid the sawyers for more sawing	13	0
Paid the joyner for worke	14	6
Paid for beere at the Reering p'te of the roofe of the church	1	0
Paid the joyner for more worke at the church	9	6
For my charges at Shrewsbury being called thither before the Committies	1	0
Given to a preacher by consent	1	6
Given to a poore man that had his howse burnt, by consent of my neighbours	2	0

Owing to the confused state of the country, and the poverty caused by the exactions of Royalists, and Parliamentarians alike, the parishioners of Tong were not as yet able to do much towards the repair of their church. The little bell had been commandeered to be melted[29] into a cannon, and the roof had no doubt been injured by lead being cut away to cast into bullets. Many such bullets made of lead have been discovered at various times in the churchyard.

On the 3rd of January 1644-45 an ordinance of Parliament took away the Book of Common Prayer and established in its stead **The Directory for the Public Worship of God in the Kingdoms**. It was not so much a Form of Devotion as a Manual of Directions. It was followed on Aug 23rd by another ordinance "for the more effectual putting in execution the Directory". By it the use of the Book of Common Prayer was interdicted not only in churches but even in private houses.

Tong Castle at the time of the outbreak of the Civil war on Aug 25 1642 was owned by William Pierrepoint, who had come to it about 1626 by his marriage with Elizabeth, daughter and eventual heiress of Sir Thomas Harris Bart. His father had been created Earl of Kingston upon Hull in 1628, and when the Civil War broke out, divided his sons between the two parties and tried to conceal himself in private life. He was, however, appointed Royalist Lieutenant General for Lincoln, Rutland, Huntington, and Cambridge early in 1643, and met his death while fighting for the king on July 25th 1643. The Earl had married Gertrude, daughter of Henry Talbot, 4th son of George, Earl of Shrewsbury. His second son, William, was born in 1607; was Sheriff of Shropshire in 1638 when he found great difficulty in collecting the Ship-money; and sat as M.P. for Much Wenlock in the Long Parliament from Nov 1640 to 1653. On July 4, 1642 he

---

[29] Bells melted -see Commons Journal Dec 8: Lord's Journal Dec 12, 1642.
By the laws of war the bells of any place captured after refusal of summons were forfeited to the master of the artillery. Charles I issued an order permitting the churchwardens and parishioners to redeem them. (Aug 7, 1643, Harl M.S.S. 6842) cf Siege of Copenhagen 1807; Flushing Aug 16, 1809. (Duncan, History of Royal Regt. of Artillery).

was appointed one of the Committee of Safety, and one of the Commissioners to treat with the king in Nov 1642, and Jan 1643. On April 10 1643 he and his neighbour, Sir Morton Briggs, of Haughton, Shifnal, were elected members of the Committee of Twenty appointed by an "Ordinance of Parliament for the Association of the Counties of Warwick, Stafford and Salop". In Feb 1644 he was one of the Committee of both Kingdoms, being one of the leaders of the Independent Party. In 1647 he was one of the Commissioners appointed to treat with the king at Newport, in the Isle of Wight, and on Dec 1 1648 received the thanks of the House for his services during that Treaty. In 1651 he entertained Cromwell at his house at Thoresby during his march from Scotland to Worcester[30]. He was elected for Notts in Cromwell's 2nd Parliament in 1656, but did not take his seat, and he also refused to be one of his House of Lords; he however sat for Notts in the Convention Parliament 1659-1661, but was defeated at an election in 1661. His death took place in the summer of 1678 in his 72nd year. He left 5 sons and 5 daughters. Of these, Robert, the eldest, born at Tong Sept. 20 1634, married Elizabeth, daughter of Sir John Evelyn, and died in 1666 leaving three sons, Robert, William and Evelyn; Gervase the third was born 1649, died May 22 1715 and was buried at Tong; of his daughters (1) Frances, born at Tong 1630, married Henry Cavendish, Earl of Ogle and afterwards Duke of Newcastle, (2) Grace married Gilbert, Earl of Clare; and (3) Gertrude married George Saville, Marquis of Halifax. His other children mentioned in the register are Eleanor bur. Sept. 1701, Margaret b.Oct 1632; Henry b. Aug 1637; William bur Nov 1640.

Of the parishioners of Tong many, no doubt, took service on each side. Some under the influence of their landlord and perhaps their own convictions, enlisting under the Parliament; others joining the Royalists. Of the latter we have the names of three. Of the six brothers Pendrill, born at Hubbal Grange in the parish of Tong and county of Salop, John, Thomas and George

---

[30] Carlyle's Cromwell's Letters, Pt.VI, letter CLXXXI, preface.

were soldiers in the first war for King Charles I. Thomas was slain at Stowfight.[31] (Thomas was sent as a prisoner to Barbados and not killed.)

Tong Castle does not appear to have been at first garrisoned for the Parliament, for among the Ottley Papers is the following undated letter April 1643 addressed

"For my much honoured Friend Sir Francis Ottley Governor. These present at Salop"

"Sir - Being informed by the Inhabytance adjoyning to Tongue Castell that the Parliamt. forces do intend suddenly to place a garrison there which will very much Anoy and prejudice that side of the country I have made bould to give you noatis of it desiring you to move my Lord Capell that there may be some means used to prevent them and if my Colonell shall approve of it I do conceive it a convenient garrison for our men till the regiment be compleat for the exercising of them, notwithstanding I leave it to your judgement, and rest Your Humble Servant,

John Holland."

Holland's advice was taken, for Symonds in his list of the Royal Garrisons in Com. Salop May 1645, says:- **"Tong Castle: First the King had it, then the rebells got it; then Prince Rupert took it and putt in a garrison, who afterward burnt it when he drew them out to the battaile of York."**[32]

---

[31] Hughes, Boscobel Tracts, p. 247.

[32] In the Mercurius Aulicus of Tuesday Nov. 21 1643, we read "the rebells in July last put a garrison into Tong Castle. Sir Thos. Woolridge, Governor of Bridgnorth, sent to Col. Leveson of Dudley that he himself would fall on Tong Castle." This attack was apparently unsuccessful. For on Monday March 25 1644 Tong was still in the hands of the Parliament on that date, since according to the Mercurius Aulicus of March 29 General Mitton drew out all the forces he could get from Tong and other garrisons to attack Lilleshall.

On Monday March 4th 1643-4 the Royalists intercepted 16 carriages laden with provisions of the Parliamentarians at Tonge, and after killing 29 of the rebells and taken 35 musketeers, brought all the waggons into Shifnal house a royal garrison under the command of Capt. Broad. (Mercurius Aulicus, Wednesday, March 20). May 3, 1644 (Friday). The forces which lay by Tonge Castle have finished their work in taking ye castle on Friday last wch was a great eyesore to his Maj' good subjects who passed ye road being in itself scarce to be taken had valiant men been in it. (Mercurius Aulicus).

It was recovered for the king by an Irish force under Colonel Tillier on April 25th 1644, and William Morris in his diary says, "1644 25th Aprilis: Tounge Castle taken." Symonds seems hardly accurate in saying the garrison burnt it when they were withdrawn. For though the "battaile of York", (generally called Marston Moor) was fought on July 1st, 1644, we know that the castle was subsequently held for the king. The references to Tong Castle, however, during the Civil wars are somewhat contradictory and confused and it is very difficult to make a consecutive history of the building from them. The garrison must have been a strong one if we may believe John Vicars when he tells us that one day (?Oct.31 1644), " Captain Stone, Parliamentary Governor of Eccleshall castle, having intelligence that the garrison of Tongue Castle were abroad, fell upon them with a party of horse, slew many of their officers, took prisoner the Governor of the Castle, and 200 private soldiers".

Another battle is alluded to in the Journal of the Parliamentary Committee at Stafford (Quoted in Shaw's Staffordshire 1.65.)

1644 April 10. Tong Castle shall be speedily relieved according to us Colonel Ruglie, Mr. Crompton and Mr. Stone shall think fit.

April 16. Ordered that £20 shall be given to the troops which is already payd to Capt. Rugeley, and a £2 of the rents of Capt. Barnsley and Mr. Draycot in Bramhurst be allowed to commanders and officers as a gratuity only to those commanders, officers and troops that did so good services in the release of Tong castle.

Tong Castle taken by Prince Rupert April 28

(Webb Memorials of the Civil War in Herefordshire - ii, 131.)

May it please your Highness

According to an order from your Highness's commissioners for the levying of the contribution I gave order for a party to be sent from Tonge Castle to Shyfnall on Sunday last to demand their contribution, having not paid any hither for the latter months. And when they came thither the Lieutenant that commanded the party enquired for the collector, who hearinge thereoff gott himself out of the church back door: then he took the constable and go-inge away Sir Morton Briggs told the parishioners itt was a shame for them to see their constable carried away with soe few a number, and encouraged them to resist, which they did accordingly, and wounded most of the soldiers, and disarmed them and called them Papish rogues and papish dogges and kept them prisoners five or six hours: and one jobber in the companie of Sir Morton Briggs chal-lenged to give battel to all the forces in Bridgnorth & Tonge, if they should come hither: and divers other out-rages were committed by them.

Desiring your Highness pleasure what shall be done in itt and that you would give me leave to wayte on you.   I am Yr. Highness most humble servant

Aug 21. 1644   Lewis Kirke

The following letter from Prince Rupert (which has been pre-served among the Ottley Papers) gives us the name of one of the governors of Tong castle for the King; and it is quite possible that Col. William Careless, as mentioned before, was for a short time another.

"Gentlemen, - Itt is knowne to you that Captaine George Mainwaring,[33] a gentleman of your owne Countrey did sometime com'and in cheife at Tongue Castle, and itt is by him signified to me that in Regard there was noe Estab-lished pay for that com'and. He was & is still unrecom-penced for his services, I desire you that he be paid out of the next contribucon comeing to the garrison of Bridge North after the proportion of five poundes a week for the time of his continuance in that com'and being from 18 July to the last of October 1644[34]. By which he may be encour-

---

[33] A Mr. George Mainwaring was a friend of Col. Careless, and was consulted by him as to means for the King's escape after Worcester.(vide Flight of the King p.212.)

[34] Again in the Iter Carolinum

1645. Oct .1   Bridgnorth Tuesday to Thursday.

Oct. 2. Dinner at Rudgeheath, the rendez-vous, supper at Lichfield, the Close.

aged and enabled to apply himself to his Majesty's farther service either in your parts or where else he shall be required. I rest your Friend Rupert – Worcester 3 Dec - 1645. Ffor the gentlemen Comrs. of the Countie of Salop, Resident in Bridgenorth, these".

(Capt. Maynwaring was apparently taken prisoner on Oct.31.1644.)

Probably Tong castle ceased to be a garrison shortly after Feb. 1644-5 since the Weekly Account of Mar. 4. 1644-45 announces that "out of Shropshire it is certified that the enemies forces have quitted divers garrisons in that county, as Rouse Castle [Rowton], Medley House, and burnt downe Tongue castle, Lea Hall and Moreton Corbet Castle, lest they should be advantageous to the Parliament"; and the Perfect Occurrences of Parliament from Friday, Aug.22 to 29 1645, includes Tong castle in the "lyst of the garrisons taken by the Shropshire Committee since they first took the field".

In 1645 Tong was honoured by a royal visit, though a hurried one - Symonds having this entry in his diary,
"Satterday, May 17, 1645. His Majestie marched by Tong, com. Salop: a faire ch: the windows much broken yet divers ancient coates of armes remaine. A fayre old castle near this ch: called Tong Castle belonging to Peirpoint this 18 years: it was the ancient seate of Stanley who came to it by marrying Vernon of the Peak at Haddon.
Thence thro' Newport."

The King was also at Tong Oct.3, 1645.

Oct. 3. Friday. No dinner at Tongue. Supper Mr. Suttons.
Oct. 4. Saturday. No dinner at Newark. Supper, Lord Danescourts.
Oct.12 .Sunday to Tuxford. Whiteheart.
Oct.13. Monday. Dinner in field at Welbeck. Supper Marquis of Newcastles.
Oct.14. Tuesday. No dinner at Newark. Supper Lord Danescourt.

The numerous marks, especially round the windows, of musket balls, with the larger one of a cannon ball, on the outside of the north aisle of the church, were no doubt made during one of the short sieges of the castle, the sacred building having been used as an outpost since it commanded the road from Wolverhampton to Newport which then ran close to the church.[35]

Though Symonds mentions the broken windows, the ancient coates of armes remained in the north and south chancel windows till Dugdale's visit in 1663. That more harm was not done to the church was certainly due to the fact that the owner of Tong estate was a strong Parliamentarian, who would naturally protect his own property, while the Royalists were not generally wont to injure such buildings since their war cry was "For Church and King."

The local legend that the shots which struck the church were fired from the castle hill at Tong Norton is proved to be groundless by the angle of impact shewn by the marks, and the distance (nearly ¾ of a mile between the hill and the church) being too great to allow of musketballs splintering the stone so deeply. According to "Norton's Gunner" (the standard work of that time on artillery, which went through many editions), the correct distance at that period to place siege guns was about 200 yards.[36]

---

[35] There is evidence that military executions in the Civil war took place on the north side of churches. At Wooton Warren, Stratford on Avon, and Kenilworth, all in Warwickshire, marks of the shot are still to be found on the walls (Sir Benjamin Stone M.P., "Popular Customs & Superstitions in Warwickshire", Lecture in Birmingham Institute Nov. 18, 1901.) But the deep dip in the road prevents us assigning this as the reason for the shot marks at Tong.

[36] cf C.C. Walker's History of Lilleshall pp 73 & 76.

Extracts from the Register 1641-46

1642   *Mr. George Meeson cleric: was buried March ye 25th.*
Rupert the sonne of Robert Bird and Anne his wife was
bap. the 12th of Jan.

1643   *Mor: Jefery Whitwicke, May the 2nd. [Will proved at Lich-*
field 1647]
Mor: Richard Harries fillius populij May the 22nd 37
Rupert the sonne of Robert Burd and Anne his wife was
buried Sept. 16.

1644   *Bapt: Charles the sonne of Robert Burd and Anne his wife*
Aug 24th

1646-7   *Bur. Thomas Duncalph March 17 [His will was proved at*
Lichfield 1647]

We shall meet with Robert Bird[38] later on, when he assisted
Charles II after Worcester. But here attention may be drawn to
his uncompromising loyalty as evinced by the names he gave
his children, Rupert after the "fiery Prince", and Charles after
the king, whose fortunes were even at the child's birth in a pre-
carious state.

Connected with Births and Deaths is the next page in the
churchwardens book, which contains **"a true & short accompte
of John Poole and Willm. Blakemore, overseers of the poor
since the 16th of Aprill 1642 untill the firste of Maye 1647,**
which is five years compleat: of monyes & goods receaved &
paid that were lefte by John Newman & Ann his wife wch. we
have releived their children withal.

---

[37] Entries such as this are common in the register of St. Peter's Church, Wolverhampton. e.g.
"Thomas the sonne of a people was baptised the last of October 1677."
[38] At the general Quarter Sessions of Shropshire held 8 Jan. 1655-6, Robert Bird of the parish of
Tong, aleseller, was ordered "to be suppressed". Possibly according to the order of the same sessions Jan. 1652-3 " that all alehouses that be presented for keeping tipplling on the Sabbath day
be suppressed".

The Goodes of John Newman were taken and
valued at   6   14   6
And the saide goodes were sowld for   7   1   0

The following extracts from the register will help to explain this

1638	John Newman and Ann Emery were marryed the 3rd of October.
1642	Thomas the son of John Newman and Ann his wife was bap. April ye 8.
1645	Elizabeth the daughter of John Newman and Ann his wife was bap. April 25.
1645	John Numan was buried June 14.
1645-46	Ann Numan widdowe was buried January 22.

The money the parents left was soon used, and for
many years the two children were a heavy charge on
the parish as is seen by the subsequent churchwardens accounts –
The overseers paid for makinge the grave and buri-
inge the corpse of Ann Newman   10d

On March 26, 1645-6 was fought the last battle of the Civil war
at Stow on the Wold Gloucestershire in which the surviving
remnant of the Royalist army was destroyed. Among those present was Thomas Pendrill of Hubbal Grange, Tong, taken prisoner and sent to Barbados.

In 1647 Roger Austen
Paid for nailes for the church doore   8   4
Paid Docetheus Twigg[39] towards the making the
church doore   15   4
Paid for beere for those that did carrie the
church doore from the castle   1   6
Paid 3 masons for 2 dayes worke in the church   7   0
Paid Thos Onians for mending the west church

---

[39] 1640. April 13. Dosythrus Twigge and Margaret Ashley married (Brewood Register).

doore   6

And in the same year **William Norton**
Paid Doce: Twigg towards the making of the
new church dore[40]   1   0   0

The Register for 1647 contains
Buried was Humfrey Duncalph, May 3 (his will was proved at Lich-field 1647)
Buried was Tho: Clarke Aug. 13 (will proved at Lichfield 1649)
Bapt was Henry the son of Robert Burd and Ann his wife. Aug 23
Buried the said Henry, Aug 30
Bapt. was Docetheas the sonne of Docetheas Twige and Margaret his wife Sept. 26.
Buried was Thomas Wolleich, gent. March 8.
This last was a descendant of James Wollrich[41], who at the Dissolution of Religious Houses in 1546-7, bought the College of Tong. On the death of Thomas Wolleich, his heirs sold it in 1649 to William Pierrepoint, owner of Tong Castle, & so it became part of the Tong Estate.

Humphry Earle in 1648 spent
Given to a breife from Ludlowe   2   0
Given to a breife on Christmas Day   1   0
Given to another for 2 decayed ministers   2   0
Given to a poore collier that had a certificate to be
read in the church   2   0
Given to a company that came out of Ireland   1   0

The accounts of Thomas Scott of Tong Norton in 1648 are very few and none of interest. In this year a windfall seems to have come to the parish for next follows this notice.
"The mony that came from Halesowen was two pounds and ffif-

---

[40] This door was probably destroyed in some attack during the Civil War.
[41] An undated list of the Freeholders of Shropshire has only two names for Tong :- Edward Stanley mil., and John Wolriche, gent. Edward S. died 1632

teene shillings". It was spent principally in "keeping Little Nu-man" (1.10.0); & in the "weekely pay of Humphrey Smyth" (18s.), though 6d. was "paid for change of clipt mony".

There are no accounts preserved for 1649, & the registers of 1648 and 1649 contain

1648   *Buried was Roger Austen July 6. (His will was proved at Lich-field 1649).*

Bapt. was Robert the sonne of Robert Burd and Anne his wife February 9.

1649   *Buried was Charles the sonne of Robert Burd and Ann his wife June 7.*

In 1650 Robert Homes

Paid for making the stile at the church yard near the Almeshowse ende	2	6
Given to one that had a breife from the Parliament to be read in the church	1	0
Given to an Irish woman that had a petition to be read in the church		6
Paid Richard Nicholas towards the paling in the church yarde	12	0
Spent in ale of those that did carrey 3 loads of timber from the p'ke feild to the church yard		3

And John Cawdwell

Given to a breife yt. P'son Chapman[42] brought to us.	2	0
Spent in beare of them that carried clay to the church yard		3
Paide Nickoles for finishinge the palings in the churchyard	8	8
Paide Thomas Harison for finishinge the Rominge of the postes in the church yard		6
Paide for makinge the church yard stile	2	4

---

[42] Rev. John Chapman, Rector of Donington 1607-1660-(ejected 1656-60). Died Dec 2, 1660, buried at Albrighton Dec 4.

1651 was an exciting year for Tong; it saw the encampment of the army of Charles II on its way from Scotland to Worcester; and shortly afterwards the defeated king and his friends were concealed by its parishioners. There are, however, no allusions either in register or Accounts to the events, unless the sermons of Oct. 5, 1651 were by a special preacher sent by the Parliament to discourage loyalty. **The churchwardens were John Baddely & Robert Clarke who kept their accounts together;** from them we take

Paide to Mr. Hilton for makinge a band for Thomas Newmon			6
Paide to William Spitel for mending the Iles in the church		2	6
Given to two pore widowes yt. come out of Ireland which had a breife		1	0
Laide out for the lead	10	12	6
For ye carrige of ye lead	2	2	6
For castinge one and thirty C. & a halfe of lead	3	3	0
For 6 daies worke for the plimer		12	0
For 12 daies for his man		12	0
Paide to Dosis Twig for makinge ye frame		2	6
For 3 daies which my man helpt to lay led		3	0
For charges and for wayinge it		3	0
My charges when I went to by lead		4	6
For tallow and grease for ye plimer			6
Given to a companie of poore which came out of Ireland which had a certificate			6
Given to an Irish gentlewoman wich had a breif ye 15th of January		1	6
Given to a distressed minister with the advise of Mr. Hilton		1	0
For 30 3 foots of nick barrie		3	9
For 2 brases for ye sance bel			6
Given to a minister which preached 2 sermons ye 5th of October 1651		5	0

In the Register the Rev. Robert Hilton, who seems to have been appointed to Tong in 1651, makes his entries from Jan 12, 1650-1 to May 6, 1651-2 in Latin though for what reason it is now impossible to say. His use of the imperfect tense in his 1st 4 entries for the burial is curious.

1650- *Richard Harrison de Tonge sepeliebatur duodecimo die Janu-*
1 *arij.*
1650 *Robertus Newman de Tong Norton sepeliebatur vicessimo tertio die septembris*
Tho: Homes de Tong sepultus fuit octavo die Decembris[43].

This thorough restoration of the church, and especially of the roof, was no doubt necessary owing to the injury inflicted during the time it was occupied by soldiers during the Civil war. The parishioners partially completed the work they were unable to perform in 1646, finally finishing it in 1671.

On March 19, 1650-1 the County Committee for Salop wrote to a Committee for Compounding. **We have several recusants' estates under sequestration.** Particulars of offers for two thirds of recusants' estates

[John] Harrington of Bishton, valued at £69	let at 66.15.0. for seven years
[Dorothy] Gifford of White Lady's valued at £90	let at 80.0.0 for seven years.
Joan Gorway of Tonge, valued at £20	let at 18.0.0 for seven years.
Walter Astley of Boningale valued at £24	let at 21.6.8. for seven years.

The nearest surname to Gorway at Tong is Robert Corwy in ch.wardens book in 1638.
Paid Robert Gorway for carriag of stone 0.11.0.

---

[43] [*Richard Harrison de Tonge sepeliebatur duodecimo die Januarij* - Richard Harrison of Tong was buried the twelfth day of January - *Robertus Newman de Tong Norton sepeliebatur vicessimo tertio die septembris* - Robert Newman of Tong Norton was buried the twentythird day of September. *Tho: Homes de Tong sepultus fuit octavo die Decembris* [Thomas Homes of Tong was buried the eighth day of December.]

1652 This year among other items of Thomas Onnions we have

Given Irishe woaman with a briefe		1	6
Pd. for makeing ye armes in the church[44]		16	0
Pd. for getting upp the scaffolde for the Paynter & takinge itt downe		1	0
Pd. for drincke which ye painters drancke		1	0
Pd. for Glasinge the church windowes	1	2	6
Pd. for fire for the glasier			4
Pd. for the glasiers diet		3	8

And among those of Robt. Blockley of Tonge Norton

Given by consent of ye p'ishe to 2 briefes	2	0
Given to ann Irishe company more	1	0
Pd. a mason for 4 daies worke belonginge to ye church at 1s. 2d. p'day	4	8
My owne wages for serving him 4 daies	2	8
To Tho: Paynton for a ffoxe heade	1	0
Pd. towards ye releife of a poore woaman which was brought to bedd in Norton	1	4

From the Register we take the following relating to the then Minister of Tong

Baptizata fuit Anna filia Roberti Hilton et Marthae uxoris ejus decimo tertio die Maii[45].

1653 Thomas Harrison enters

Disbursed for bread and wine at Whitsuntyde	2	10
For my labour to fetch it		6
To a petition from Ruatt	2	6
To a breife belonging to a minister in Wiltshire	1	6
For bread and wine for a communion at Christmas	3	2
To a breife concerning Malbrudge	8	4

Received of Sarah Onyons for breaking the Ile	2s	6d

---

[44] I.e. those of the Commonwealth, ordered to be put up in 1651.
[45] [Anna, daughter of Robert Hilton and Martha his wife, was baptised the thirteenth day of May.]

Received of those yt pay noe leowne at the collection for Mal-
bury   1s. 8d.

**While his fellow warden, William Hardweeke of Tong Nor-
ton, disbursed among other payments**
To Malburrow   5   0
ffor a loud of coules and carriage for Wid. Minshall   10   0
To a distressed minister   2   6
ffor sett. John the sonn of John Price an app'tic.   5   0   0

1653 Thomas Onyons de Tonge sepultus fuit decimo quarto die Julij[46]

**In 1654 the churchwardens were Thomas Scott and George
Holmes, the former**
Paid for wine for a communion   3   6
Paid for bread for a communion   2
Paid for thesching widdow minshawes howse & for
getting the broome for it   3   8
Given to a ministers wife that was in greate disstres   8

The latter
paid the money that the ould church wardens
borowed of Humphrey Earle.   4   0
Given to a man with one hand with a breife
Paid William Spittle for mending the iles   2   0
Paid Mary Cooke for beare that William Spittle had   2

1655 this year we have only the accounts of **Robert Owen**, his
entries include
Given to a strange minister by consent   2   6
Payd to an Irish woman with a briefe   6
Received of a stranger for breaking the ile in the
church   6   8

In the Register we find the name of the person buried in the

---

[46] [Thomas Onions of Tong was buried the fourteenth day of July.]

church

Mr. Pedley, of the parish of Blimhill, was buried at Tong September the 4th 1655.

Issabell, the daughter of Robert Hilton and Martha his wife, was bapt. Feb the 14th.

Thomas Mayer, Clarke of the parish, was buried the 22nd of Feb.

In 1656 John Bennett served for Tong and William Blakemore for Tong Norton. Bennett spent

For relieving and lodging five Irish men and women with a pass	1	0
For cutting briers and brambles offensive to the church		6
To a man with a petition for a collection for a greate losse by fier given by consent	4	0
For bring a booke appoynting a day of humiliation and twice with quarter money to the High Const: to Donington[47]		4

In the registers for 1656 we find no entries of interest, but in **the accounts of William Blakemore**, churchwarden for Tong Norton, we find he charged for his journeys of half a mile to Tong.

My charges to Tong at divers times uppon church busines	6
To William Skerrington for ringing	6

1657 Edward Poole and George Meeson were churchwardens and overseers this year.

In **the former's** accounts are

June 2	ffor the cariage of a waine load of cooles ffrom peanes lane for the widdow minslow	4	0
July 5	Given to a minnister with consent which preached two sermons	5	0

---

[47] This was the general fast day ordered by Cromwell when he heard of the determination of the Duke of Savoy to make his subjects return to the Roman Church, and that all who refused were massacred. A national contribution for the relief of the sufferers was also ordered. Milton at this time wrote his sonnet "On the late massacre in Piedmont".

Aug. 20	Paid two masons for covering two graves and mending two other plasese of the church alies and for mending one arch of the north side	2	4
Nov. 18	Given to a man and his wife which came out of ire land with a certificate of greate losse		6
Dec. 10	Paid Dotheus Twigg for reparing an ould dore for the west end of the church	2	6
	Paid for a peece of timber 6 foote longe to Docetheus Twigg		4
	For nailes for the saide west dore		5

On the other hand **George Meeson** enters

Given to a pore distressed widdow wich had grete lose bey fire	1	0
Given to a pore distressed womman wich came from Ireland	1	0
Pide to the carpinter ffor mending the curch yard gate and belongeing to itt	2	0
Pide to Doziey Twigg for timber and workemanshipe for the mending of the curch yard stile	2	4
Given to a distressed seeman wich had a brife		6

From the registers we take

Elizabeth the wife of the Hon. William Pierrepont of Tong Castle, Esq. was buried July the first.

John Evans of Tong Norton and Mary Parker of Bishupbury were married the 12th of June, before Mathew Morton, Justic of the Peac.

From the above extracts we learn that Pains Lane (now better known as St. George's) was a colliery district 250 years ago.

Elizabeth Pierrepoint was the surviving daughter & heiress of Sir Thomas Harries Bart, who brought the Tong Estate to her husband William Pierrepoint.

In 1653 an order was made that all marriages should take place before a justice, but this is the only one entered as such in the Tong Register.

In 1658 the churchwardens were **William Cope and Thomas Martin** but their accounts contain no item of interest, nor any entries in the register worth transcribing except perhaps this
Nov. 18 Gerard Thurston, of Newport and Ann ffrith of Wolverhampton married by Mr. Tho: Challener.[48]

In 1659 William Norton of Lyzeard Mill and John Smith of Ruckley Grange held office.

The former enters

To the clerke for scouring the gutters	4
To the clerke for ridding the church	6
For mending the comunion table	2

The latter gives us the clerk's name

To Humfray Mear for clensing gutters	4
For ridding the church	6
For burying a poore beggar	4
Given to a poore man with a pass of request	6

From the Register we take
Elizabeth the daughter of Richard Nicholls and Margaret his wife was baptised in the font the 4th of March by Rob: Hilton then minister of Tong.

In this year we have the second (cf 1653) notice of the use of the legacy left by Lady Harries for apprenticing poor children – "memo: That Thomas Sutton the soone of Thomas Sutton was put out an apprentice to Richard Ford in the yeare 1659: for to mainetain him and teach him his trade he recd. £5. 0s 0d.

In 1660 we find no reference in either Register or accounts to the Restoration of the monarchy. The wardens were Thomas

---

[48] This Thomas Chaloner, the ejected headmaster of Shrewsbury School, who was headmaster of Newport Grammar School from January 1656-7 to his return to Shrewsbury in 1662.

Scott and Humphrey Earle. The former enters

For one jornye to Much Wenlock	1	0
For goinge three times to Bridgnorth being commanded concerning the Dole mony	3	0
The latter		
Paid for a rope for the great bell and tags	5	0
For sendinge a warrant to Kemberton		2
For goeinge to Muchwenlock being comanded	1	0
For goeinge four times to Bridgnorth	4	0
For a rope for the clock	1	6

In the Register for 1660 we find for the first time entries of collections in church for briefs, i.e.
On May 13th- 8/11 for Southwold, Suffolk, and on Aug. 25th- 5/10 for Willenhall, Staffs, but a full list is given at the end of these notes.

The next year **(1661)** there are no churchwardens' accounts preserved the only entry being
Richard Ford, one of the churchwardens for the year 1661 had put into his hands by the parish at his entrance 13/10. Martaine Wheler his fellow warden recd. at the same time 6/0.
But on the fly leaf of the Register is the following note.
"Memorandum: Aprill ye 29th 1661: Put in a coffer in the vestre, (Thomas Harrison being yt day made clerke) one Church bible, one Hommile booke: two bookes of Disputatio betwixt Harding and (blank): a Pulpet cushion: and two blacke Cloathes; and the pariphrase of Erasmus".
The following briefs are mentioned in the Register, on April 28, 4/- for John Davies of Herefordshire; Ilmister (July 14) 5/-; City of Oxford (Aug 4) 7/-; James Mulnill (Aug 18) 3/2; Quatt 4/2d; and Motheringham 3/6d.
This year "William Yarsley, sone of John Yarsley," was apprenticed for 7 years to George Bird, "sumaker" of Shifnall, the money being £5. 0. 0.

In 1662
Humphrey Earle and William Scott held office.

Given to a poore man that had great losse by fier and had letters of request from Trentham	2	0
Paid to the Aparritor for a booke & bringinge of it.	2	0
Given to a minister that was in want	5	0
Laid out at the Archbishops visitation and my charges that day	4	0
Given to a breife for the repaireing of Gravesend church, the charge being valued at 2525li	5	0
Paid for washing the surplis		6
Given to tow poore men that had bin prissnors		6

William Scott expended

Given to a sowldier that came by passe			6
Paid ffor a surplus & makinge thereof	2	3	0
Given to a poore scoller that came with a certifiecate from the deane of Chester			6
Paid for a dore for the steple & a cover for the font		4	2

Nathanael, son of Roger Hampton, was this year apprenticed to Thomas Brooke of Lapley, shoemaker.

Shropshire Quarter Sessions, April 1662, the east end of Cosford Bridge ordered to be repaired "at the cost of Tong Allotment".

In 1663 we have the first entry of the Election of the Church-wardens at the Easter vestry given

"Memorandum: that upon the 20th day of Aprill in the yeare of our Lord God 1663 Mr. William Salter and Edward Holmes weare elected church wardens for the p'ish of Tonge by us whose names are subscribed" (6 signatures follow).

Edward Holmes, among other items

Pd. Tho: Harrison for cutting the briars from aboute ye church	6

Pd. for an houre glasse		9
Pd. for a booke of canons	1	0
Pd. for a proclamation for ye Sabbath's better obser- vation	1	0
Pd. the Visiter for the exhibition of a copy of the paesh [? R'gestr.]	1	0
Pd. the Visiter for exhibiting a copy out of the procestr	1	0

William Salter

Pd. for a booke of Articles	1	0
Pd. for a proclimation relating to the better observa- tion of ye Lords day	1	0
Pd. for a roape for the snts bell	1	0
Pd. quarter money at Christtide	4	4
Pd. to Dositheus Twigg for worke about the pulpit	4	0
Pd. for a Justices warrant against Timo: Gregory		8
For my owne charges at Bridgnorth	1	0
Pd. for 2 more warrants directed ag'st Timo: Gregory		8
Pd. to a man for goeing with the said Timothy to Bridgnorth	1	0
My own charges upon the same occasion	1	0
Given to a poore man yt came from Lidbury		6

1663 April 24 Lucy Hodgkiss, daughter to a poor man, that dyed at the White Ladys, buried.

Sir William Dugdale, Norroy King of Arms, was at Tong Church in September 1663, when making his Heraldic Visitation of Shropshire. He records that in the south window of the chancel were (1) the arms of Pembruge impaling Lingen. (2) of Pembruge, (3) Lingen, (4) Fitzalan, (5) Vernon, (6) Vernon, (7) Pype, and (8) De la Bere. And in the north window was (1) Trussel impaling Ludlow, (2) Ludlow impaling Lingen,(3) Ludlow impaling Vernon, (4) Lingen, (5) Pembruge, (6) Pembruge impaling Lingen, (7) Vernon impaling a blank, (8) De la Bere impaling Fitzalan. These have all entirely disappeared. Dugdale also describes the monuments, saying of the Stanley tomb that the inscription on it was written by Shakespeare – (Harleian M.S. 5816 foll. quoted in Eyton ii pp 250)

On June 6, 1663 Charles II, gave as a free gift "ye sums of 100 li in full of an order of 200 li to be equally divided amongst" William Pendrill, Richard Pendrill, Humphry Pendrill, John Pendrill and George Pendrill. The receipt (which is in the Salt Library, Stafford) bears the marks of all, except Richard, who on June 24, had given Francis Coffyn power of Attorney to act for him, Richard describes himself as "of Hobball Grainge, in the County of Salop, yeoman".

Upon the 11th day of Aprill **1664 Robert Homes and Robert Blockley** were elected churchwardens and of the 7 who signed, the first name is that of Joseph Bradley, Minister, whose earliest entry in the Register seems to be on Feb 24, 1660-1.

Robert Holmes

Paid Mr. Bradley for copping out the register		6
Paid the parriter for carring it to Litchfield	1	6
Given to one hungerford a gentleman beggar		4
Given to 3 women whose husbands weare prisoners under the Turks		8
Given to a breife for a bridge in Norhamptonshire	2	0
Given to a breife for a church in Northumberland	2	0
Paid Mary Cooke for lodgeing 5 Irish gentlewomen	1	8
Paid the parriter for a booke for keeping the 5 of Aprill holliday	1	6
Paid Spence the mason for mending a breach that was falne in the North Ile		6
Given to two companies of Irish gentlewomen	2	0
Paid the parriter for a booke of artickles	1	6

The accounts of Robert Blockley have not been preserved.

1664 Indenture between Wm. Pierrepont and Robert & Edward Bird.

In a volume of still unpublished M.S. by Sir Wm. Dugdale is a passage dealing with **the Stanley monument.** After quoting the prose epitaph in full Dugdale continues. "Shakespeare [in the margin]. These following verses were made by William Shakespeare, the late famous tragedian". Dugdale's text is followed by a series of drawings of Shropshire antiquities made by Francis Sandford, and in Sandford's sketch of the Stanley monument at Tong we see the pyramids with their finial balls and spikes in their original position; the allegorical figures, now sadly defaced and banished to the niches on the arch dividing the Vernon Chapel from the south aisle, standing on the canopy; and the whole composition from the side, a view which, wedged as the tomb now is between the earlier Vernon monument, it is today impossible to photograph.

1665. Memorandum: That upon ye 28th day of March 1665 **John Baddeley, senior & John Cooper** were elected and chosen churchwardens of the p'ish of Tong (here follow 6 signatures). Of these **the former** includes in his accounts

Paid to Samuel Grise[49] for worke aboute a tome	16	4
For sharpeinge his Tules for that worke		9
Paide to ye pareter for a booke for the fast day[50]	2	0
Paid to ye arch dekein's pareter	1	0
For mendinge the clocke	1	0

---

[49] A note by Lady Elizabeth Wilbraham in a book at Weston Hall referring to the above Samuel Grice is as follows
"For Building Weston House, 1671.
Sam; Grice agreed to gett ye stone at ye Knole for 18d. a yard.
To hew for 1s. a yard.
To lay it being carried within 40 yards distance 1s. per yard.
And for ye inside brickworke 6d. a yard.
For foundation worke 18d. a yard."
[50] The fast day was connected with the terrible outbreak of plague in London, caused probably by the exceptionally hot summer of 1665. A proclamation of July 6th ordered that Wednesdays should be kept for prayer and fasting and that collections should be made for the poor who were "sick and visited" with the affliction.

Paide for 2 mates for the parson   8

Give to too souldiers which were hurt   6

He also gave on 8 other occasions to those in distress a total sum of 8/4.

John Cooper has

Given to a man that came out of Lancashire with a letter of request   2   0

Given to one Catherne Winter that came with a letter of request   6

There is also the following regulation as to **fees.**

"October 4th. Memorandum. It was then agreed betwixt the Minister and the churchwardens for ye p'ishe of Tonge that ye fees of the churche due to the Minister should bee paide as in King Charles hys tym the firste, that is to say foure pence for the interring of eyther man or woaman and foure pence for the Churching of a woaman. And this was agreed unto in the p'sence of us whose names are here subscribed.

Willia: Scott. Tho: Lateward. William Salter. George Meeson. John Homes. John Evans."[51]

1666 Memorandum that upon the 17th day of Aprill in the yeare of our Lord God 1666, Robbert Clarke & Edward Bird weare elected churchwardens of the p'ish of Tonge (8 signatures). The former however since he was an R.C. did not serve, and the entries for this year are headed "The Accompts of **Mr. Edward Bird**, Sole Churchwarden and Overseer of ye poor in Anno. 1666"

Disbursed by mee on one journey to Litchfeild   4   2

Pd. for two bookes of prayer   4   0

Pd. for mendinge the paynt howse over ye church

---

[51] As the first three are styled Mr. or Gentleman in the Register, and the people of those days were not very lavish of such distinction, we may safely infer that they were among, if not the, principal parishioners.

yard gates		7
Pd. to Anthoney Spicer for killing a fox in our p'sh.	1	0
Pd. to John Paynton for makeing a besam	1	0

Anthony Spicer was at this time living at White Ladies, in 1707 he became a parishioner of Tong. Probably the "two bookes of prayer" were in connection with the **great fire of London**, which beginning on September 2nd reduced the city from the Tower to Temple Bar to a heap of ashes. On September 13th a royal proclamation commanded Wednesday, October 10th to be observed by all "as a Day of Solemn Fasting and Humiliation, to implore the mercies of God, that it would please Him to pardon the crying sins of this nation, those especially which have drawn down the last and heavy judgement on us, and to remove from us all other His judgements."

1667 Memorandum. That upon the 9th day of Aprill in the yeare of our Lord God 1667 Thomas Harrison and William Hardwick were elected churchwardens for the p'ishe of Tonge.
(8 signatures, including Richard Warde, minister, whose handwriting appears 1st in the Register on May 11, 1666.)
Thomas Harrison

Gave to a breife concerning the Loss at Newport	8	4
Paide for a warrant to bring the ffidler before the justices		4
My charges at Bridgnorth when we brought the ffidler before the justices	1	0
Paid for a second warrant for to bring the ffidler before the justices		4
My charges at Bridgnorth	1	0
Paid to John Horton for mending the Iles	2	1
Gave to a poore man of the p'ishe of Quat wch. had suffered greate loss by fier	2	0
Gave to a man that had a certificate of greate loss at sea		1
Paid for mending the Pulpitt cushion	1	0

Paid the parrater for a booke of Artickles   1   6

"Robert Blockley, who served for William Hardwicke,"
Gave to a breefe concerning the loss at Newport   8   4
My charges at Bridgnorth when we brought the ffidler before the justices   1   0
My charges going with the ffidler before Sir Humphrey Brigges   4
My charges at Bridgnorth going to make returne of a warrant concerning the fidler   1   0
Paid for a warrant at the same time   6

The "parrater", or apparitor, it has been suggested was the parish beadle. The word has a wide use (it is of course derived from *appareo* to appear) and was applied to the man who carried summonses, whether in civil or ecclesiastical courts. Latterly the name has been confined to the latter.

1668 Memorandum: that upon the 24th day of March 1667, Robert ffoster, gent, and George Homes were elected churchwardens for ye parrish of Tonge, to serve for ye yeare 1668 (7 signatures)

George Homes
Paide to Doci: Twigg for setting ye admonition concerning marriage up in church   4
Jan. 10. given to a minister that preached heare twice that day   4   0
Paide for a rope for the greate peease   2   8
Given to a man of our county that had suffered greate loss by fier   4   0

Robert Blockley who served for Mr. Robert fforrester churchwarden
Given to three widdows that had a letter of request published the 27th day of ffebruary   2   0

My charges when I brought the certificate to the high
Constable concerning the fier at London   4
In a deed of 1680 Robert Forster is described as "of Tong Norton in the parish of Tong", while ffrancis Forster in 1684 signs
one "relating to land etc. in Tong Norton in a common street
there". The latter had married Mary daughter of Thomas Scott of
Tong Norton, who died in 1652. Francis Forster, gent, sold his
interest in Ruckley Grange in 1691 to Goldsmith Mills. In 1634,
when he bought Ruckley from Sir Robert Vernon, he was described as "of Sutton Maddock". The Forsters in a contemporary
document are called "a good old family of Papists" and in a list
of Shropshire recusants 1581-2 is the name of Humfrey Forster,
gent, of Tong Norton; and on July 11, 1690, orders were given to
sieze and bring to the town of Shrewsbury as a recusant and
suspected person Robert fforrester, of Tong, gent.

*There are many prints of Tong castle. This bas-relief shows Durant's rebuilding. At
one time it was part of the wall at the entrance to one of the carriageways to the
Castle. It now stands in the church porch, where it is easily viewed.*

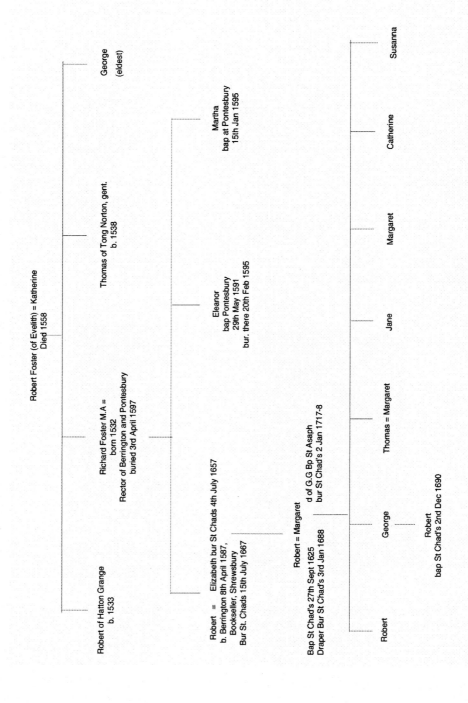

Robert Foster (of Evelith) = Katherine
Died 1558

Robert of Hatton Grange
b. 1533

Richard Foster M.A =
born 1532
Rector of Berrington and Pontesbury
buried 3rd April 1597

Thomas of Tong Norton, gent.
b. 1538

George
(eldest)

Robert = Elizabeth bur St Chads 4th July 1657
b. Berrington 8th April 1587,
Bookseller, Shrewsbury
Bur St. Chads 15th July 1667

Eleanor
bap Pontesbury
29th May 1591
bur. there 20th Feb 1595

Martha
bap at Pontesbury
15th Jan 1595

Robert = Margaret
Bap St Chad's 27th Sept 1625
Draper Bur St Chad's 3rd Jan 1688

d of G.G Bp St Asaph
bur St Chad's 2 Jan 1717-8

Robert

George

Thomas = Margaret

Jane

Margaret

Catherine

Susanna

Robert
bap St Chad's 2nd Dec 1690

In 1662 a most important change was made in the Poor Law of 1601 by the creation of the law of Settlement. By this law any labourer coming to seek work in a strange parish might within four days be removed back to his own parish, unless he took a tenement over £10 a year in value, or gave security that he would not become chargeable to the parish rates. There are many of these bonds preserved in the Tong Parish Chest, the earliest of which is dated May 20, 1668. This is the bond of Thomas Leland, husbandman, and his sureties were Humphrey Pendrill of Bloxwich parva, Staffordshire, yeoman, and George Pendrill, of Hednesford, Staffordshire, yeoman.

1669. Memorandum: that upon the 13th day of Aprill 1669 Robert Wooer, and John Evans were elected churchwardens to serve for this yeare 1669 – (10 signatures)

Robert Owen

Payd for an houreglass for the church	1	0
Given to a man with a letter of request 13 in number	1	0
Given to a souldier and his company		6
Payd for washing the sarplice and the Cloth for the Communion Table	1	6

The bond of Richard Williams of Pattingham, Staffordshire dated July 10, 1669, bears the name of "John Pendrill, of Albrighton Shropshire, husbandman". This John was the 2nd of the brothers and lived at White Ladies in 1651, as a kind of woodward there; according to Father Huddleston, he took the most pains of all the brothers. In addition to the 100 marks granted in Aug. 1663, Charles II, by a warrant dated Nov. 9, 1674, gave him a further reward of £200 for his good and faithful services. After the Restoration he lived at Beamish Hall, Albrighton.

1670. Memorandum: that on the 5th Day of Aprill 1670 Wm. Cope and Robert Blakemore were elected churchwardens to serve for this yeare 1670 (11 signatures).

William Cope

Paide William Blakemore for mending the light gates		4
My charges at Leitchfeild at the Quarter	1	0
Paide Thomas Sutton for drawing straw for the widdow Painton		10
Paide the thatcher and his man	1	8
Paide for the straw that thatched the widdow Paintons house	5	0
Paide for glasing the greate window in the west end of the church and for mending the other windows in the church	3 0	0
Paide for washing the Tablecloath that was borrowed for the communion table at Easter	1	0

Robert Blakemore

Given to the Captine and his company with a pas[52]		4
Given to foure souldiers with a pas		4
Paide the parrater when hee scited us to Leitchfeild	1	0
My charges at Leitchfeild at the courte	1	6
Given to a man in Hales p'ishe with consent	1	0
Paide for carrying barrels for the sawyers in to the parke		4

"In the yeare 1670, John Paynton, the sonn of John Paynton, was sett an apprentice to a pewterer in London ffor wch. Was pd. By Mr. Will: Scott tenn pounds being p'rishe mouney.

George Harrison ye sonn of Tho: Harrison was at ye same tym sett an apprentice to London to a bricklayer ffor wch. Was given by Mr. Will: Scott seaven pounds tenn shillings wch. Was parrishe mouney.

Disburst by Mr. Will: Scott of ye P'rishe mouney unto Mary

---

[52] Probably the Captain, and the soldiers were on their way to join the army which was to co-operate with the French forces in attacking Holland. This was according to the Secret Treaty of Dover which Charles II made with Louis, by which he agreed to declare himself a Roman Catholic on condition he should receive a large sum of money, and a share of Holland when it had been conquered.

Paynton the daughter of Mary Paynton to have her toucht by the kinge for the Evill the summ of forty shillings.

Disburst by him unto John Sutton ye sonn of Widd. Sutton of Tonge Norton for the like occasion ye summ of forty shillings."

1671. Mem: that upon the 25th day of Aprill 1671 ffrancis Homes was elected churchwarden for the Township of Norton.

Mem: that upon the 25th day of Aprill 1671 William Cope was elected churchwarden for the Township of Tonge, by us whose names are subscribed; who doe faithfully p'mise unto him, the said William Cope, that when it shall by Due Course fall next to be served by the house he now liveth in, he shall be exchused by reason at our request hee serveth two years together now. (7signatures)

Interior of the church with three decker pulpit from an etching of S F Every 1841.

This year the church underwent much restoration, probably not having been thoroughly renovated since the injuries of the Civil Wars. The money spent comes to £40.18.0.

William Cope (among other sums)

Pd. for a new stile for the churchyard		8	0
Pd. for falling, squaring, & cutting a tree in ye p'ke for boards & other timber		6	0
Pd. for sawing sixteen hundred and forty foote of sawing for the church bords and other timber	1	12	9
Pd. for makeing a sawepitt			10
Pd. our charges when wee fetcht ye leade		2	0
My charges at Leichfield when I went to bargaine with the plummer		1	6
Pd. Thomas Owen for carrying two loads of timber for ye parke		1	0
Pd. Robb. Potts for turning ye boards		1	0
Pd. to Timothy Gregory for waying ye leade		1	0
Pd. my expenses when we sould the ashes		1	0
Pd. for thirteene hundred and 3 quarters of leade to Mr. Holleys	9	2	0
Pd. the plimmer for casting and laying ye leade	4	15	0
Pd. Docytheus Twigg for worke doun at ye church	2	0	0
Pd. Docy. Twigg for mending ye moulde to caste the sheets of lead and two stricklesses		1	6
Pd. Docy. Twigg for 2 daies worke aboute getting the leade upon ye churche and ordering the winde to gett the leade upp withall		2	0
Given John Smyth when hee went to gett his pension		2	0
For my owne labour for carrying of three loads from ye Castle to ye church of leade		1	0

Copy of the original churchwarden's accounts, taken from microfiche. Not all the £ s d have reproduced. It shows how Auden only selected the parts he thought most interesting. Permission of Shropshire Archives.

Thomas Harrison "who served for ffrancis Holmes", (among other sums)

Pd. for carr. two loads of timber out of the p'ke to ye church	1	0
Pd. for carr. one loade of Kidds from ye hoult	1	0
Pd. for carr. 9 loads of leade and one loade of latts to ye Castle	3	0
Pd. John Horton for makeing a ffurnace for the Plymmer	1	0
Pd. cutting and carr. 3 loads of wood for the plimmer	1	0
Pd. for carr. 2 loads of leade more to the castle		6

Pd. for Ridding ye house where ye plimmer caste ye leade			6
Pd. for carr. 3 loads of leade from the Castle to ye church		1	0
Pd. for carr. two loads of leade more from the Castle to the church			6
Pd. for ale for the plimmers			6
Pd. for coles yt ye plimmer had to melt withal lead for Sowther for the leades			6
Pd. Mr. Holleys ye plimmer	4	0	0
Pd. for fetching and bringing ye fforge waites to way the leade withall			6
Given to Timothy Gregory for waying the leade ashes			6
Pd. for carr. of two loades of sand from ye Knole		1	0
Pd. the mason for worke doun at ye church	1	6	8
Pd. ye glasier for mending the church windowes		3	0
Recd. For lead asshes: seaven hundred waight	1	8	0

In this year 1671-2 died Richard Pendrill, of Hubbal Grange, of a rapid fever, at the house of Mr. Henry Arundel, in the parish of St. Giles in the Fields, London, where he was buried. The following is the epitaph on his monument there.

Here lieth
Richard Penderill
Preserver to His Sacred Majesty, King Charles II of Great Britain, after his escape from Worcester fight in the year 1651, who died Feby. 8.1671.
Hold, Passenger, here is shrouded in this hearse,
Unparallel'd Pendrill through the Universe,
Like when the Eastern Star from Heav'n gave light
To three lost kings, so he in such dark night
To Britain's monarch, lost by adverse war,
On earth appeared a second eastern star,
A pole astern in her rebellious main,
A Pilot to his Royal Soveraine;

Now to triumph in Heaven's eternal sphere
He's hence advanced, for his just steerage here,
Whilst Albion's chronicle, with matchless fame,
Embalms the story of great Pendrill's name.

William Pendrell of the parish of Tongue and Jane Jelligoe of Codsell Wood were married 18 of Nov. 1671 (Newport, Salop, Register)

1672. Memo. That upon the 9th day of Aprill 1672 George Meeson & Thomas Painton the younger of Tong Norton were elected churchwardens (7 signatures)
There are however no entries of interest in George Meeson's accounts, but the following from those of "Will Blackmore whoe served churchwarden for Tho: Paynton of Norton," shews that Tong Norton paid a separate assessment for church rates.
Rec: two brownes for Norton   £2.6s.8d.

This year we have the bond of Thomas Carpenter, nailor, dated March 3, 1672, one of his sureties being George Carpenter, of Tong, locksmith (see 1670); and also another mentioning John Cooper, senior, and John Cooper, junior, "of Bisshopp's Wood, in the parish of Tong and county of Salop, husbandmen". This latter dated Nov 30, 1672, shews that the wood extended into Tong parish in former times & explains the entries "of the Wood", and "de silva", in the Register. In a map of 1739 the present White Oak farm is called the Wood Farm.
1673. Memo. That upon the 1st day of Aprill 1673, John Smyth, of Ruckley Grange, and Will: Norton, both of the p'sh of Tonge weare elected churchwardens for the yeare ensuinge (8 signatures)

John Smyth

Paide for a quarter and halfe of lime	4	6
Given to William Blackemore for vewing the steeple		2
Paide for a ridel for the lime		4

Paide for haire and for carrige			3
Paide to Will: ffellips for liker for ye steeple		1	6
Paide John Horton for chuseinge quores			1
Paide to Thomas Owen for a fox hed		1	0
Paide for a Motto to keene of the gifts that the Lady Harris gave to this church		13	8
Paide to John Baddely for a hooke and thimble for it			6
Paide for a frame for the Motto		4	0

William Norton

Paide to the masens for pointeing the steeple	2	1	6
Paide for a voider for the plais			6
Paide to John Horton for layinge quores in ye church		1	3
Given to them which reared the laders			6

1674. Memo: that upon the 21st of Aprill 1674 Edward Poole of Tonge was elected churchwarden; and Elizabeth Martine widd,[53] to find an able and sufficient man to serve the office of churchwarden in her sted for the yeare ensuinge (5 signatures)

Edward Poole churchwarden and overseer enters

May 28. pd. for makeing a bier, for neels, for worke and four small peeces of timber	4	4
Nov. 6 pd. for a cloth and a napkin of diaper for the communion table	11	8
pd. for makeing and washing them		6
Jan 3. paid for paper for the pulpitt cloth		1

Robert Blockley "serving for the Widdow Martin of Tong Norton, churchwarden and overseer", enters

Given to a minister in distress	4

---

[53] Elizabeth Martin was one of those instrumental in saving the King in 1651. Buried at White Ladies 21 Jan, 1707-1708

1675. Memo. that uppon ye 6 day April 1675 was elected ffrancis Homes for Tonge, and Thomas Harrison for Norton churchwardens for the yeare ensuing, ffrancis Homes serving for Gorst House. (7 signatures)

Among the payments of **ffrancis Homes**, churchwarden and overseer are

My charges at Shifnall at the monthly meitting		4
Given a poore seaman with a pas		2
Given a poore souldsure with a pas		1
Given a poore distressed minister		4
Given a poore seaman with a pas		1
Given a poore minnister		4
Oct. 28. My charges at Shroosbury to give account of the Recusants' estates	2	6
Given a distresed minnester		4
Pd. the parreter for a booke	1	6
Given a memed souldear and a wife with a pass		4

Among those of **Thomas Haris**, churchwarden and overseer, are

Pd. for sining the Return of the inhabbittance Impoyable of the chimne mune[54] of our parishnors	6
My charges that day at Shifnall	6

In the yeare 1675 Charles Smith the sonn of Thomas Smith of Tonge Norton was sett an apprenttis to John Whistons of London, of Sengoyles in the feeleds, Joyner, for the which he received tenn pounds from the hand of Mr. William Scott being parish monney

By letters patent, July 24, 1675, perpetual pensions were assigned to

Mary, widow of Richard Pendrill, and Richard Pendrill's heirs	100	0	0

[54] Chimney money, or hearth money, was a duty imposed by 14 Car.ii 1662 of 2s. for every hearth in a house, a most unjust tax (see Adam Smith "Wealth of Nations" Bk.V.ch ii. pt. 2). It was abolished soon after the revolution of 1689. Pepys writes "March 3, 1662. I am told that this day the Parliament hath voted 2/- per annum for every chimney in England as a constant revenue for ever to the Crowne."

William Pendrill and his heirs	100	0	0
John Pendrill and his heirs (100 marks)	66	13	4
Humphry Pendrill (100 marks)	66	13	4
George Pendrill (100 marks)	66	13	4
Elizabeth Yates	50	0	0
Total	450	0	0

The pension of Mary Pendrill, relict of Richard Pendrill, and her heirs, was a grant of the annual payments due to the crown from the lands at Lilleshall, formerly the property of the Abbey and other places.

1675-6 Jan. 6. Grace Carelesse buried. She was the widow of Francis Carelesse, the nephew of Colonel William Careless, who assisted Charles II in 1651. The Anne Careless who was buried on Dec. 15, 1701 was possibly her daughter.

1676. Memo.that uppon the 28 of March 1676 wee doe elect Tho: Lateward and William Scott churchwardens for the yeare ensuing. (8 signatures)
There are, however, no more churchwardens accounts entered in the book, though their elections are continued to 1682 and briefs are mentioned till 1680.

In this year by order of the Archbishop of Canterbury **a religious census** of his province was made. The return from Tong of all the "inhabitants above the age of 16" was "Conformists 156, Papists 13, Nonconformists 0". And on comparing this with the other parish returns we see that there were more Roman Catholics at Tong in proportion to the population than in any other parish in Shropshire. The Pendrills of Hubble Grange, the Clarkes of Lizard Grange and the Fosters of Ruckley probably account for this.

1677. Memo. That uppon ye 17 day of Aprill 1677 wee doe elect

Richard fforde and Martin Wheeler churchwardens for the yeare ensuinge. (6 signatures)
In the yeare 1677 "William Hope the sonn of John Hope of the parishe of Tong was putt an apprentice to a Surgeant Barber in the Citty of London. Given with him aleaven pounds".
"Pd. in the same yeare for the curinge of two children of Mary Payntone widdow of scaldheads sixteene shillings six pence".

1678. April 2 1678. Elected churchwardens for the parrishe of Tonge for the yeare ensuinge William Salter for Tonge, William Scott for Norton for his lands there. (8 signatures including William Cotton, curate who first enters in the Register on May 1, 1677).

"On Dec 7 1678 an order was made by the House of Lords for leave to bring in a Bill to exempt **the brothers Pendrill** and certain others, in consideration of their service in the preservation of his late majestie Charles the second, after the late battle of Worcester, from being liable or subject to the penalties of any laws relating to Popish recusants". (Flight of King p. 329) (To save them from inclusion in Titus Oates Plot).

In the summer of this year the Right Hon. William Pierrepoint, Lord of Tong, died at the age of 71. He was not however buried at Tong though his wife had been in 1657. After the injury to Tong Castle in the Civil War he seems to have resided at his Nottinghamshire estate of Thoresby, where his younger children were born. He was succeeded at Tong by his son Gervas.
1679. There is no account preserved of the election of churchwardens for this year, but the **accounts of Nathaniel Myveart are on a loose sheet of paper in the church chest**, where also are some accounts of 1684, 1685, 1686, 1691 and 1711.
Nathaniel Myveart disbursed among other sums

Wyer to mend ye clocke	1	0
At my Lord Bishop's Visitation paid toward a new booke	2	3

ffor a new church wicket	6	0
To a distressed captain with his Maje'tis privy seal given		6
ffor mending the clock and diall	1	0
John Baddeley's bill for necessaries for the church and church yard	5	2
ffor stocking of the Treble Bell	6	8
ffor mending ye Great bell stock	5	0
ffor iron work for ye Treble bell	2	11
Masons work for the use of the church	4	2

The bills for the last five items have been preserved loose in the chest.

1. Feb. 9, 1679: received then of Nathanael Myveart one of the churchwardens for the p'ish of Tong, the sum of six shillings eightpence for stocking ye treble Bell, and five shillings for mending the Tenor Bell stock; in full discharge of all accounts betwixt me, John Hackett of Newport, carpenter, and the said Nathanael Myveart from the beginning of the worke to the day of the date thereof: summa   11   8

2. Worke for the parrish:- for iron worke for the Trebel bel   2   0

for a clipe, and iron weges and coters and big neles for the fift bel   8

for neles   3

Some   2   11

3. John Horton's Accounts: 1 day for repairing ye church wickett, and pointing ye fflashes round about ye porch and over Mr. Pierrepoints pue, and for pointing ye fflashes on ye backside of ye church, and ffor laying a grave: 2 days ffor myself 2s.8d.; 1 day for George Daws 0s.10d.; 1 day for George Painton 0s.8d = 4s.2d.

Hackett's bill, when compared with the churchwarden's entry, shews that some of the former references to the great bell may refer to the Tenor Bell and not to Sir Henry Vernon's Big bell. Horton's shews that the Golden Chapel was the Castle pew and was known as such in general talk. On the dissolution of the College of Tong, an annual rent of 12s. 11d. "for Vernon's Chauntry in the church of Tong" was paid to the King. (Staffordshire Archaeological Society's publications 1884)

Deeds relating to Tong in a second hand catalogue

1680. Deed between Robert Bill of Stanton and Robert Forster of Tong Norton in the p. of Tong.

1684. Deed between Bartholomew Dippery of Liddiard in p. of Idsall in co. of Salop, relating to land etc in Tong Norton, in a common street there, with signature of Ffrancis Forster.

1716. Deed between Thomas Tomlinson of Tong Norton and Richard Marryon jun. of Tong, relating to land called Bentley in Tong. Signature and seal of Thomas Tomlinson.

1717. Deed between Richard Marryon jun. of Tong and Elizabeth Viccars of Church Eaton, and Obediah Blockley of Tong relating to land etc. in Tong, bought by Tomlinson, with seal and signature of Rich. Marrion.

1722. Duke of Kingston and Thomas Pemberton, of Tonge Norton in ye p of Tonge, gent. relating to land etc in the manor of the p. of Tong with signatures of T. Pemberton, Thomas and Elizabeth Scott and most noble Evelyn, Duke of Kingston, relating to land etc in Tonge and Tonge Norton with signatures of Thos. and Eliz Scott.

1723. Thomas Scott of Tonge in co. of Salop, gent. and Elizabeth Scott and the most noble Evelyn, Duke of Kingston, relating to farmhouse, land etc. in Tonge Norton in co. of Salop, with signature of Elizabeth Scott.

1724. Duke of Kingston, Richard Marryon and others relating to lands etc. in Tong, signed by Marryon, Wheeler and Blockley.

1731. John Poole, of Meosell in the p. of Tonge, and Elizabeth nee Reynolds, and Richard Darling, of Codsall, co. Stafford, relating to land etc in Meesel, with signature and seal of Richard Darling.

1717. Deed between Richard Whiston of Kilsall, in co. of Salop, relating to land etc. in Tong Norton, with signatures.

1738. Deed of Richard Beech, of Tong, in co. of Salop, yeoman, relating to land etc. in Brewood, co. Salop.

1746 William Barker's account of manors of Tong and Tong Norton.

1747. His account for this year.

1809. Map of W. Yates shewing the Red House – opposite Kilsall.

1680. upon Tuesday, the 13th day of Aprill 1680 wee doe elect churchwardens ffrancis Homes and Robert Blockley for the yeare aforesaid. (six signatures)

1681. April the 5th 1681, then was John Baddele and John Cowp elected churchwardens for the yeare ensuinge. (3 signatures)

1682. Elected April 18th 1682 Ralph Adeny churchwarden, and Avis Clarke to finde a sofishient man to serve churchwarden for

the parrish of Tonge for the yeare ensuinge. (8 signatures)
Avice Clarke of Lizard Grange was a strong Roman Catholic
and so a recusant.

Robert Blockley and George Harrison churchwardens
1683. *November 1, Lott, a ffoundling child, baptized.*
This child cost the parish a considerable sum for those days. In
the churchwarden's accounts of **1685** is the entry
Pd. to Dorothy Yeate the 11th of June for the Bastard   £1.0.0.
And in the church chest is the following bond.
June the 11th 1684. It was then agreed betwixt the present
churchwardens of Tong, and Dorothy Yates as followeth:
Imp. Dorothy Yates doth agree with the churchwardens aforesaid that she, the said Dorothy, shall take and keep one younge
man child whose name is Lott, & to keep him with meat, drinke
and all other conveinences for and during her naturall life and to
reseave foure pounds of lawfull mony of England in manore &
forme as followeth:
That is to say twentie shillings upon her recait of the child, &
twentie shillings that day twelve moneths, and twentie shillings
the 12th of June which will bee in the yeare of our Lord God
1686, and the last twentie shill: to bee p. to her the 12th of June
1688: and this wee agree to. Witnesse our hands the day and
yeare above written in presence of

William Scott	Robert Blockley
Tho: Lateward	George Harrison
Edward Poole	Churchwardens
Richard Blakemore	the mark of
	Dorothy X Yates her marke

And pinned to this receipt.
June the 11th 1685. received then of the Churchwardens and
Overseers of Tonge the sum of one pound upon an agreement
made betwixt the churchwardens of Tong and me the yeare
1684.
I say received By me 1.0.0. Dorothy Yates X her marke.

1684. The accounts of George Harrison one of the churchwardens and overseers of the pore for the p'ish of Tong 1684 have been preserved. They include

At the visitation for Mr. Cotton's dinner		6
For mending the surplice		3
Pd. to ye Parrittor for the Proclamation	1	6
Pd. to Francis Sandland for mending ye bench in ye bell house		7

The bond mentioning Thomas Sutton, of the Wood, in the parish of Tonge, and co. of Salop, husbandman, is dated July 31, 1684.

1685. The accounts of both churchwardens for this year have been preserved in the chest.

Thomas Owen

Pd. for a booke for the 29th of May	3	0
Pd. part of the fees att the Buishops visitation	2	6
Payd for a warrant to bring in the feffees	1	0
My charges that time		6
Payd for John fox his horse		1
Pd. for a Booke for the 30th of January and 6 of ffebruary	3	0
Pd. for Counsell about Sara Overton	5	0
ffrancis Homes and my owne charges going to Oakengates	1	0
My charges going to Dawley	1	0
For neeles to mende the church coffer		1

John Evans

Pd. to 7 travelars with a pas the 5th day of August that came from Ireland			4
Pd. for a book at the visitation the 18th of Sept.		1	0
Pd. for going to the Justice for a warrant for the faithfees			6
For going to the Chancelors visitation		1	0
Pd. to Dorothy Yeate for the Bastard	1	0	0

On Lady Day 1685 **the pension of £100 granted to John Rogers** and Anne his wife was 3 months in arrear, and that of £30 to Ann Bird was also in the same condition. John Rogers had married Ann daughter of Richard and Mary Pendrill of Hobbal; (the "Nan" whom the King had taken on his knee). Ann Bird was either wife or daughter of Robert Bird of Tong, one of those who were instrumental in preserving the life of Charles II prior to his arrival at Bentley Hall.[55]

1686. The accounts of **Robert Blakemore** for the yeare 1686 still exist, they include

for fetching a warrant for Thomas Gollins		1	0
paid for the warrant		1	0
for going before the Justice with Thomas Gollins		1	0
pd. to Robert Scholey	1	10	0
pd. to Dorothy Yeate for keeping of Lott		10	0

The bond of John Horton, of the Heath, in the parish of Tonge & county of Salop, Mason, is dated Dec 14. 1686-7.

There is also a bond, dated Sept. 16. 1686, between Thomas Rogers of Tonge Mill, in the co. of Salop, miller, and Robert Scholey and Robert Blackemore, churchwardens and overseers. It is to this effect: **Thomas Rogers with his wife and family is admitted into the school-house in Tonge,** there to abide until some other place is provided for him, his wife and family to inhabit. If they then depart peaceably & quietly out of the school-house as soon as some other habitation is provided, and leave behind all such Locks, Keys, Bolts, hinges, doors, glass, glass-windows and other things as do belong and appertain to the said premises, without any troubles, delays, molestations, suits, disturbances whatsoever, the present obligation is void and of none effect. But if otherwise, Thomas Rogers must pay £40 of good and lawful money. It is witnessed by Fenihouse Lees, John Baddeley, and the Rev. William Cotton.

---

[55] Flight of King p. 328, 331, 332.

1687. Order of Quarter Sessions, July 1687. The case of Anne Roe, referred to Brimstree Justices. She is with child by Nathaniel Wall, she and he being servants to Roger Roden of Tonge.

1690. On July 11, 1690 orders were sent to Capt. Thomas Ottley that he should give command "to his officers and troopers to seize or cause to be seized and brought to the towne of Shrewsbury such Papists as may be suspected to be disaffected to the Government". Those in "the Brimstrey hundred were Edward Revell, of Shifnall, gent, his nephew --- Revell, John Sowtherne, of ye White Ladyes, gent, and Robert fforester of Tong, gent."

The Rev. George Plaxton, Vicar of Donington writing about 1690 says "Lyziard Grange still enjoys great privileges. The tenant can, at his pleasure, take in and hold for his tillage a good part of Tong Heath, which is known by ancient banks and ditches".[56] In King John's Confirmation Charter the gift of Lyziard Grange is called "the land of Lusghart between Watlingstreete, Merdiche & two rivulets". Lizard Grange is bounded to the N. by the old Watlingstreet Road, to the E. and W. by two small brooks, & very probably had a ditch for its meer or boundry to the S. tho' none such can now be traced.[57]

1691. The accounts of both churchwardens are still in existence
Thomas Scott ye churchwardin of Tonge Norton.

pd. to Anthoney Spicer for squaringe a tree and sawing 212 foote of boarde	5	6
pd. for cloth to make John Horton cloaths	7	0
pd. for 2 dusen of buttons and 3 peneworth of thrid		7
pd. for makeinge them	1	6
pd. Rogar Roaden constable ye quarter pay	3	10
pd. Mr. Goodwin for Mary Paintons soar legg the 29th of March 1692	4	0

---

[56] O & B. ii. 537.
[57] O & B ii. 265.

pd. to six maimed souldiars yt wher maimed		6
pd. Thomas Wenlock cunstable ye quarter pay	3	4

Richard Marion

Paid for a box for ye church	0	4
pd. for 2 shirts for Jno. Horton and makeing ym	2	10
pd. for makeing a pair of Britches for Jno. Horton and mending a pair		9
pd. for Inkle for Jno. Horton		½
pd. for a pair of shoes for Jno. Horton	2	0
pd. Mr. Goodwin for salve for Mary Peinton, junior	4	2
For washing the surpliss and communion cloaths	1	6
For scowdering the plate		2
pd. to make too shirts for the French boy		4
pd. Jno. Adey for mending 2 windows in ye church	3	9
pd. for a rope for ye clock	1	7

Recd. by ye churchwardin of Tong Norton 4 lewns wich come to	4	13	4

1692. A bond, dated Dec 6, 1692, mentions William Gyles, yeoman, Henry Gyles, yeoman, John Sotherne, yeoman, Margaret Gyles, daughter of William Gyles, all of the White Ladies in the co. of Salop, and Thomas Sutton, of the Wood, in the parish of Tong, in the co. of Salop.

*1694. March 27, **William Scott** buried.* A slab to his memory was discovered in 1892 bearing the inscription "Here lyeth the Bodyes of W. Scott and Eliz. his wife. He departed this life March ye 24th ano. dom. 1694 in the 73rd yeare of his age. She the 30 of October ano. Dom: 1700 in ye 80 yeare of her age". The Scotts were owners of Cosford .[58] Two deeds of 1723 are extant (1) Between

---

[58] see 1639, and S.A.S.T. vol. IX series 2, in the History of Albrighton.

Thomas and Elizabeth Scott and the most noble Evelyn, Duke of Kingston, relating to land etc. in Tong and Tong Norton with the seals and signatures of Thomas and Elizabeth Scott; and (2) between Thomas Scott, of Tong in the co. of Salop, gent. and Elizabeth his wife and the most noble Evelyn, Duke of Kingston, relating to a farmhouse, & land etc. in Tong Norton, in the county of Salop, with the signature of Elizabeth Scott.

1694. The following **Bellringers rules** hang at the bottom of the steps leading up to the Belfry, whither they were removed from the outside of the pillar by the order of Bishop Lonsdale.

> If that to ring you doe come here
> You must ring well with hand and eare
> Keep stroke of time and goe not out
> Or else you forfeit out of doubt:
> Our law is so concluded here
> For every fault a jugg of beer.
> If that you Ring with Spurr or Hat
> A jugg of beer must pay for that.
> If that you take a Rope in hand
> These forfeits you must not withstand,
> Or if that you a Bell o'erthrow
> It must cost six pence 'ere you goe.
> If in this place you sweare or curse
> Six pence to pay, pull out your purse,
> Come pay the Clerk it is his fee
> For one that swears shall not go free.
> These Laws are old, and are not new
> Therefore the Clerk must have his due.
> *George Harison. 1694.*

1695. The bond of Henreay Millward, late of the parish of Roster, and Bridget his wife, is signed by Thomas Pendrill, of Kiddimore Green, in the parish of Brewood, and co. of Stafford, yeoman. It is dated July 13. 1695.

1696. On a loose sheet is the following memorandum:- "1696, 8th Jany :- For Planting 4 Trees"; but there is nothing more. It may possibly refer to the yew trees, of which there are four, in the churchyard.

1697. August 31.
Elizabeth, daughter of Hon. Gervais de Pierrepont and Lucy his wife, buried.
This was the only child of Gervas, Lord Pierrepont and Lucy his wife, daughter of Sir John Pelham, of Sussex. Over the vestry door is a marble monument to her memory with this inscription.

Hic intra
Terrestria Impedimenta
Praematurius reliquit quasi ad coelum Properans
Elizabetha Pierrepont.
Ao. Aeroe Chrni.C I Ɔ I Ɔ C X C V I IPridie Kal. Sept.
Annos nata XI
Puella ingenii acuminis & Morum Urbanitatis
Supra Aetatulae captum. Quam multa jam Feliciter edocta,
Nihil non si diutius Parcae Favissent Assecutura
Parentum Decus Dulce Familiarum Deliciae
Utrorumque spes gratissima
Filia unica Gervasii Pierrepont Armigeri Dni Terrae de Tong
Nepotis Roberti Pierrepont Comitis Kingstoniae
Acerrimi (ingruentibus sub Carolo Io. Rege dissidiis Civilibus) Strategi
Fidelitatis suo Principi debitae, etiam vitae dispendio Assertoris:
Cui Genus ortum a Roberto de Pierrepont
Gul'mo Io Regi Expeditionem Comite;
Fratrum natu maximo,
Quorum etiam dum superest in Normannia
Posteritas.
Όν γ'σ φιλει θεοσ γ' αποθνησκει νεος⁵⁹.

---

⁵⁹ [TRANSLATION (not supplied by Auden but taken from George Griffiths, "History of Tong and Boscobel" page 93):   Here, below, Elizabeth Pierrepont prematurely has cast off (her) earthly trammels, as it were hasting to heaven, in the year 1697 of the Christian Era, on the day before the Kalends of September (31st August) Eleven years old. A maiden endowed with a mind, prudence and sweetness of manner far beyond her tender years: How many precepts of her parents would she not have gladly followed if the Fates had spared her longer! The ornament of her friends, the delight of her family, the most pleasing hope of both: the only daughter of Gervase Pierrepont, Esquire, Lord of the Land of Tong, nephew of Robert Pierrepont, Earl of Kingston, in the civil wars which raged bitterly in the reign of King Charles I, the asserter of

Owing to her death her father gave the following gifts to Tong.

1697. On Oct. 23. 1697, (9 Will. iii), a deed was drawn up between the Right Hon. Gervas, Lord Pierrepont, Lord of the Mannor or Lordship of Tong, in the co. of Salop, of the one part, and Sir Humphry Briggs, of Haughton, in the co. of Salop, Baronet, Thomas Jobber, of Aston in the co. of Salop, Esquire, William Scott, of the parish of Albrighton in the said co., Batchelor in Divinity, Robert Moreton, of Shifnal, in the said co., gentleman, and Thomas Hatton of Tong, in the said co., gentleman, of the other part.

Income for the Minister of Tong and the Poor of Tong

It is to the following purport:- For the better maintenance of such person as at the death of Lord Pierrepont should be minister or curate of Tong, & his successors, & towards the relief of certain poor people of the same parish, the said Lord Pierrepont gave, confirmed, & conveyed all the tithes, or tenths of hay, wool, lamb, hemp, flax, apples, pears, & all other tithes, oblations & offerings whatsoever (the tithes of corn and grain only excepted) growing within the aforesaid parish of Tong, and the town fields, limits, precincts, and titheable places thereof, unto the above mentioned trustees upon trust immediately after Lord Pierrepont's death to permit the minister of Tong & his successors to have and enjoy of the said tithes & premises with their appertenances for ever. He further granted six several annuities or yearly rents of £30; £14; £6; £12; and £10 making together £84, issuing out of the manor of Tong, with the appertenances in the co. of Salop, and out of the Castle of Tong, to be paid by half yearly payments at or on the feast of the Annunciation of the Blessed Virgin Mary, and St. Michael the Archangel by even

---

fidelity due to his Prince, even at the cost of his life: He was descended from Robert de Pierrepont, companion of the expeditions of William I, the Conqueror - the eldest brother - whose posterity even yet survives in Normandy.

Whom God loves dies young.]

and equitable portions, to commence after the decease of Lord Pierrepont. The annuity of £14 to be paid for or towards the defraying the yearly expense of diet of or for the minister & his successors. The annuity of £6 to be for or towards the yearly expense of keeping one horse or mare of the said minister, with however this proviso for any Lord or proprietor of the manor of Tong who should reside at Tong Castle, and sd diet the minister of Tong for the time being, at his or her own table, and should allow him hay for his horse at any time from Bartholomew-tide to the 10th of May next, should retain to his or her own use the annuities of £14 and £6 a year for every year that he or she should so diet the minister & keep his horse, and in proportion for any lesser space of time. And the annuity of £12 to be paid to the Minister and Overseers of the poor of the parish of Tong, to be by them yearly distributed among 6 poor widows to be placed by the Lord of the manor of Tong for the time being in the almshouses at Tong, everyone of them to have yearly 40s. apiece. And also the second annuity of £12 to be employed by the Minister and Overseers, and laid out in buying Staffordshire wool, and in the yearly setting at work the poor people of the parish of Tong in the manufacturing it into cloth, & to the further purpose that the Minister and Overseers should yearly distribute among the 6 poor widows so much of the cloth as should be sufficient to make them 6 gowns yearly, the remainder of the cloth not wrought up into the gowns to be distributed among the poor people of the parish of Tong other than the 6 widows at the discretion of the Minister & Overseers. The said annuity of £10 to be employed in buying hemp and flax and in the yearly setting to work the poor people of the parish of Tong in the manufacturing the same into cloth, to be yearly sold for the best price, and the yearly income to be employed by the Minister and Overseers in the placing out of such poor children of Tong, whose parents shall not by the Minister and Overseers or the greater part of them, be thought able to maintain them, as shall seem convenient to be apprentices with whom they shall think fit. Also one other annuity of £30 to be paid half yearly to the Minister of Tong, at such times as the Minister could not enjoy the aforesaid tithes with this proviso that the said minister should not enjoy or claim the said tithes and annuity together, but the one or the other only. And for the better accommodation of the Minister and his successors, they should at the decease of the said Lord Pierrepont, hold and enjoy for ever one chamber in the aforesaid Castle of Tong, the uppermost chamber up the back stairs there, as the same was then furnished with books and presses on both sides, together with the usual free and uninterrupted way or passage to & from it and also the free and full use of all the said books and all such others as Lord Pierrepont should during his life appropriate to the use of the minister and his successors; and the better to ascertain the said books it was intended that a catalogue should be made and Lord Pierrepont would thereto subscribe his name. Also such minister should for ever have and enjoy the free and uninterrupted use of part of the stable for the keeping of a gelding or mare with a place over the same for keeping hay, and also at every tide and times between May 10, and Michaelmas Day should graze and depasture the mare or gelding in Tong Park without any interruption or payment. But should the minister be unable to enjoy the use of the stable, another yearly rent of 40/- should be paid to him, and also a further yearly rent of 40/- should he be unable to enjoy such grazing and depasturing in Tong Park, and a further yearly rent of £5 in lieu of the use of the chamber in Tong Castle, and Lord Pierrepont granted another and further annuity of £100 to be forfeited out of the Castle Manor lands so often as the books before mentioned or any of them should at any time after the death of Lord Pierrepont be taken away or disposed, so that the minister for the time being could not have the use of the said books, and the owners or proprietors of Tong should not upon notice supply and make good such books so taken away; the trustees receiving the forfeiture of £100 should, subject to the supplying such books taken away, render the overplus to the proprietor of the manor of Tong. Further when the trustees mentioned should by death be reduced to 2, then the survivors should elect 5 others sufficient and proper persons to be trustees for the tithes, annuities and penalties granted by this deed.

1697. About this time there are several entries of **persons residing at the White Ladies** being buried at Tong viz.

1697 Nov. 20. Griffith Tolley, of the White Ladies.
1697-8 Jan. 2. Judy Giles of the White Ladies.
1698 Sept. 23. Magdalen Mary, of the White Ladies.
1699 May 7. Elizabeth Brook, of the White Ladies.
1699-00 Jan. 21. Mary Yates, of the White Ladies.

While on the other hand two parishioners of Tong were buried at White Ladies, viz 1698, June 20, Isabella Duncalf; and 1700, Aug. John Rogers.

Apparently the Protestant inhabitants of White Ladies were buried at Tong, and the Roman Catholic parishioners of Tong at White Ladies.

With reference to some of the former, the Rev. George Plaxton, Rector of Donington 1690-1703 makes this entry in the Donington Register: "All at ye White Ladyes, and all in one house aged now 272 years, 92 Henry Gyles, 93 Judith Gyles, 87 Griffin Torry. Memorandum yt Henry Gyles died in ye yeare 1694".

1700. Aug. At the White Ladies, John Rogers, of the parish of Tong buried.

This was the son in law of Richard and Mary Pendrill of Hubbal, by his marriage with their daughter Ann, who was nursed by the King in 1651. He apparently lived at Hubbal himself.

In the London Post with Intelligence Foreign and Domestic cf. August 19-21, 1700, is the following statement:- "We have advice from Staffordshire that one **Pendrell** (being the last of the family that was instrumental in saving King Charles II by hiding him in the oak ever after called the Royal Oak, after the battle of Worcester), has departed this life; but that which makes his death very remarkable is that on the very day and hour that he died, the said oak was blown down by a storm of wind."

This must refer to William Pendrill who was living at the age of 84 in the reign of William III.

1701. On a loose paper is the following entry

"1701. pd. for a Black Cloth for a Bier   1.15.0."

"The old church [at Weston] was pulled down April 1700. The foundation of the new church began to be laid on ffriday, May 3rd. 1700. The new church was first preached in on St. Andrew's day, Novemb. 30th 1701. This new church was erected at the proper cost and charges of Dame Elizabeth Wilbraham". (Weston Parish Register). Lady Wilbraham employed at least one Tong man in the work, for in one of her books she makes the following note "Mr. Pereponds Joyner offers March 1701 to Wancote ye Cherch att Weston for ye rates underneath," & then follow his charges.[60]

1707. The bond of Anthony Spicer "of the Aunccient Extraparochiall of White Laydyes" bears the names of Richard How; Thomas How; Thomas Howe, junior; and Richard Pendril, all of the same place. It is dated "ye 3rd of January ye 6th yeare of the Raigne of our Soveraigne Laydie Queen Anne, Annoque Dni 1707."

A small piece of paper inscribed "Southwell Church in Nottinghamshire Ao. 1713"

gives a list of those who subscribed to the brief

	s	d		s	d
John Cotton	0	3	Richard Ore	0	1
George Holmes	0	2	Thomas Blakemore	0	2
Mr. Rogers	0	3	Mr. Cowper	0	3
John Rannalds	0	1	Ld. Pierrepont	2	0

---

[60] Historical Collections of Staffordshire Vol.ii (new series) p 309.

Robert Holmes	0	3	Lady Pierrepont	2	0
Richard Duncalfe	0	2	Mrs. Montague[61]	1	0
Mr. Scoley	0	3	Mrs. Metcalf	1	0
Francis Harrison	0	2	Mr. Pietier	0	6
Mr. Blockley	0	3	G. Oswald	0	6
Richard Beach	0	1	Mr. Duncalf	0	2
Mr. Salter	0	3	R. White	0	1
Thomas Salter	0	1	Mrs. Baker	0	4
John Baddeley	0	3	Mr. Hutton	0	2
			Total	10	9

This is written on the back of part of a letter ending with these words: "So wishing you all health and happinys, your ever duti-full son till death, R. Holmes – London. May ye 16-1713."
and "Docter Sacheverill[62] is apointed to preach before ye house of Commons upon ye 29th Instant."

Another loose fragment bears the following
Offerings   Dec. 25. 1713.

	s.	d.		s.	d.
Mary Yearly		6	Jone Newman		4
Mary daws		4	Elizabeth Parker		4
Margeret Smith		4	Samuel Parker		6
Sarah Rathbone		4	Als Smith		4
Mary ffox		4	Ann Smith		4
Francis Peinton		4	Mary Bainton		6
Sarah Gollins		4	Jos. Answel		6
Mary Lateward		4	Susan Sutton		4

---

[61] The above mentioned Mrs. Montague was Mary, daughter of Evelyn, Duke of Kingston, and great niece of Gervase, Lord Pierrepoint, who had married Mr. Edward Wortley Montague on Aug. 12, 1712. She was born in 1690, and died Aug 21, 1762. Her father succeeded to the Tong estate on the death of his uncle in 1715. Lady Montague was an authoress, and introduced inoculation for smallpox into England.

[62] "Dr Sacheverell, for two scurrilous intemperate sermons, very undeserving such exalted notice was impeached at the Bar of the House of Lords (Dec 13 1709) and sentenced not to preach for three years" O. & B. vol 1 chap xii, page 501-3. He was appointed Rector of Selattyn and made a royal progress on his way there especially in Shrewsbury.

1715, April 22. This day, at about 9 aclock in ye morning, there was a total **eclipse** of ye Sun, so near being total yt ye whole globe of it appeared to the eye wholly hid, which lasted above two minutes. Several stars appeared, and everything look'd much darker than in ye twilight; insomuch yt ye largest Prints cou'd not be read in open fields; nor hardly any Body be seen in Houses.

"June 18. Ye Rt. Hon. Gervase, Lord Pierrepont buried."
Lord Pierrepont was buried in the Stanley vault within the altar rails, and till the Restoration in 1892 a small brass was in the centre of the sacrarium bearing the inscription "The Rt. Hon. Gervas, Lord Pierpoint, Baron Pierepont of Hanslop, county Bucks and Baron Pierepont of Arglas in the Kingdom of Ireland departed this life May the 22nd 1715 in ye 66 year of his age." This brass was moved close to the north wall. When the vault was opened in 1892, his coffin was found bearing the inscription on a lead plate "The Rt. Hon. Jervos Lord Pierpont, died May 22nd 1715."

In the chest is the following notice of a **Court Leet**, the first no doubt held after his death.
"These are to give notice That the Court Leet, and Court Baron, of the Right Honorable, Lady Lucy, Dowager Pierrepont, for her Mannor of Tong, will be holden at the usual place, upon fryday the twenty first day of this instant month of October, by tenn of the clock in the forenoon of the same day – at which court all persons who thereto owe suit and service and all the said Ladies Tenants are required to give their attendance – dated this 5th day of October 1715."

An order dated Jan. 6th, 1714-15, settles Mary Yates of Brewood, who had "served as a hired servant with one John Rogers of Hubbuelle in ye p'rishe of Tonge for one whole yeare and halfe and received fourtty five shillings for her yeare and halfe wages," as a legal parishioner of Tong. Further references to her will be found in 1719.

In 1716 a list was published of the Roman Catholics who in 1715 refused to take the oath of allegiance to George I. [Here] are found the names of John Rogers of Hubbald Grange; Robert Collingwood, priest, of Boscobel; Thomas How, of Boscobel, and many of the Pendrill family. An order in Council dated April 6, 1716 exempted the descendants of those eminently instrumental in preserving Charles II after Worcester, from penalties as Popish Recusants (see Flight of King, pp 329, 330) including this John Rogers, and Thomas How, and the Pendrills.

Occasional Notes in the Register.
March ye 14th, **1716-7.** It began to **snow** at 5 o'clock in ye afternoon; and without any intermission continued till noon ye 16th. Though a strong wind blew all ye while, yt drove ye snow into hollow Places to so great a height as to make ye roads altogether impracticable, yet was ye snow upon ye level in ye garden behind ye Castle found at least 13 inches deep, and sixteen in ye court before it. It did snow again and freeze excessive hard all ye next night, and ye night following. A vast number of sheep were buryed under ye snow, 20 or 30 and more of ym together. The sheep yt lay buryed five or six daies escaped, but those which continued longer under were found dead. So great a snow in so short a time, and in a season so far advanced had never been seen by any body in ye Parish. It occasioned, as it had done ye year before, a mighty bright Meteor in ye air, in ye night, some few daies after it had wasted away.

Sept. ye 10th, **1717.** The moon happened then to be totally eclipsed at six in ye afternoon; but ye weather proving foul at yt very time, ye **Eclipse** was hardly perceived.

A small paper document describing the beating of the bounds at Tong in 1718 was found by the Rev. H. G. de Bunsen at Donington and sent to the Rev. R. G. Lawrence, Vicar of Tong, on

Nov. 20th 1872. It is however no longer to be found among the Tong papers, and the following transcript is taken from Mr. G. Griffiths' *History of Tong* pp 132, 133.

The 19th and 20th of May in Anno 1718. Memorandum, the days and year above written being Rogation weeks, a Boundery of the Lordship, or Mannor and Parish of Tonge was then taken by the Minister and such of the Inhabitants thereof whose names are hereunto subscribed, and is as followeth:-

Impr. It was begun at Tonge Mill Poole and went Eastward up A Brooke called Kilsall brooke unto a Bridge over the said brooke in the road from Tonge to Albrington on the midle of which Bridge was a Gospel Read.

And from thence Eastward up the aforesaid brooke unto the upper part of a piece of ground in the tenure of John Cotton, called the Healds, from thence across the bottom of widdow Harrison's fieald unto the corner of Tonge Parke pale, then forward adjoyning to the lands of Will. Colemore Esq. in the tenure of John Yate and Thomas Ellits, four foot on the outside of the Park pale all along, likewise from thence forward on the outside of the Park pale adjoyning to the lands [of] Ffitchherbot Esq four foot, being in the tenure of Thomas How adjoyning unto the Park pale up to the Keepers meadowes, then continuing on by a bond hedge made by Mr. How from the Keepers meadows, and also from the Parke fields, from thence unto a marle pitt in Mill field in the tenure of Mr. How, being adjudged to be an acre which formerly paid tythes to Tonge, thence returning out of the grounds of Mr. How into Ambling meadowe and still continueing by Mr. How's bond hedge unto Morell's meicell now in the tenure of John Carpenter to a gate place there where there was then A gospell read.

And from thence along by the bond hedge of Dennis Field, in the upper part of the aforesaid field is about two acres of land in the parish of Tonge and pays tithes to the Lord of the

Mannor of Tonge as often as it is tilled, from thence returning out of that lande into Bryery hurst and still continuing by Mr. How's bond hedge unto Pierce Hay lane, thence returning to a gate entering into Bishops wood where there was then A gospel read.

And from thence by a bond hedge dividing from the parish of Brewood, leading to a piece of land, Pertry leasow, in the tenure of William Leeke, and from thence by a bond hedge dividing from the parish of Blimhill untill we come to Weston Parke Pale corner, at a gate there was then a gospel read.
Then goeing seven foot of the outside of the Weston Parke pale westward unto a piece of land called Cowe haye, then continuing by the Bond hedge of cowe haye in the Parish of Weston unto Cowe haye gate where there then was a gospell read.
And from thence continuing by the Bond hedge belonging to Weston parish aforesaid unto a certain gate leading of Norton heath unto Weston new Mill where then there was a gospell read.
And from thence by the aforesaid Bond hedge of Weston unto Windrill meadow, and from thence continuing by certain grounds called the Windrills unto Street way still by the parish of Weston along certain grounds in the tenure of John Fox of Lizyard grange unto the road from Tonge to Newport where there was a gospell read.
And thence along the lands of John Fox aforesaid adjoyning to Street road in the parish of Sheriffehalse, unto a certain brooke runing from Burlaughton in the Parish of Sheriffhalse, and from thence southward downe by the said Brooke adjoyning to the Parish of Shiffnall alias Idsall unto a way and steping stones upon the same Brooke below Thomas Wenlock's corne Mill where there then was a gospell read.
And thence along the same brooke unto the upper forge hammor ditch where there was then a gospel read.
And from thence along the fforge brooke unto a way and

steping stones where was then a gospel read.

And from thence by the same brooke to a bridge below the lower Forge where there was a gospel read.

Thence by the same brooke unto Timlett Bridge where there then was a gospell read.

And from thence by the same brooke unto a certain bridge over which is a way into Muncke fields from Ruckley Grange near below which bridge is a bylott or spot of land over the brooke belonging to the parish of Tonge adjoining to a meadow in the holding of Lancet Jones, then returning to the Forge brooke aforesaid downe to a bridge below Ruckley Grange house upon which there then was a gospell read.

And from thence along the same brooke to the Hole, upon a bridge there then was the gospel read.

And from thence by the same brooke round to Ruckley wood cornor, which is the tenure of Thomas Scott, untill it meets the Brooke that runs from Tonge Mill: thence returning up Tonge Mill brooke adjoyning to the parish of Dunington, untill we come to a certain Piece of Land about halfe an acre lying over the said brooke, now in the holding of John Horton, which is in the Parish of Tonge, unto a gate upon Worcester Road where there then was a gospel read.

And from thence returning two and up the saide brooke untill we come to Tonge Mill, at a gate over the poole Bridge adjoyning to the Parish of Dunnington where there then was a gospel read.

And the Boundary there ended.

Lewis Peitier, curate of Tong.

George Salter
Robert Homes
Richard X (mark) Marrion
Roger X (mark) Mason
Thomas Ore
John Cotton
George X (mark) Holmes

The seavon of the Jury at the Court Leet & Court Baron held for the Mannor of Tonge the 26th of Oct. 1719, know the Boundaryes.

[John Auden once lent some of his notes to J. H. Clarke. At Mr Clarke's death Mr. Clarke's papers came to John Auden who wrote – "These notes were founded on some loose memoranda which I lent him, and his own recollections of the place. The notes were found among his papers at his death in a motor accident on 8th April 1931." Some of these notes (which now follow) give more information about some of the people and places mentioned above.

Beating the Bounds

Signatories	Names	mentioned
Lewis Peitier buried 1745	Widow Harrison	Buried 22 Feb. 1732
George Salter buried 1737	John Fox	Lizard Grange bur. 1733
Robert Homes buried 1728	Thomas Wenlock	Lizard Mill
Roger Mason buried 1728	John Horton	Old Bell Inn near Church
Thomas Ore buried 1729		
John Cotton buried 1732		
George Homes buried 1729		

The Street Way – or Street Road, called Streetway Road is Watling Street.

Tong Mille Poole – Humphry Pendrell's Mill below Tong Castle. This was kept by a family of Rogers in the 18th century who were descended from the Penderels of Hubbal, (a Roger married a Pendrell). A Rogers was moved from there to a portion of Tong College.

Corner of Tonge Parke Pale – The land was not disparked till later "E.P.L.D.K." on Tong Park House.

White Oak – a large oak formerly white washed to mark the way through the forest into the old bridle road to Albrighton.

The Meicell – Meese Hill – a labyrinth – a path through dense undergrowth. The "Maze" hill.

Dennis Field – still owned by Boscobel owners who still pay 6s. per annum tithe to Tong Manor. Probably from St. Denys – France's patron saint – who possibly might have some special devotion given him at St. Leonard's Priory. The bridle path field and one adjoining bear the names of "White Ladies' Close" and "Minerals Leasow." Also "Ore's Bank" and "Little Ore's Bank" from an Ore who farmed them. "Pertry" or Pear Tree Leasow still so named south of Park Pale House.

Cowe Haye gate – a haye – the fenced or paled part of a forest into which beasts were driven to be caught.

Norton heath – the unenclosed land from Tong Norton to Cowe Haye wood – on the Mere side – Moors, Bentleys etc.

Tong Heath – the unclosed tract of land between the Blacklands and Burlaughton Corner.

Stoneyford – Burlaughton – now styled "Burlington".

Weston New Mill – This may have been recently erected, for the old windmill close to Streetway was in existence in 1686.

The Windrills – fields west of the Woodlands farmhouse still retain the name.

The names of *Upper Forge Hammer, Forge Brook, Lower Forge etc.* refer to the fact of the iron works once there.

Up. For Ditch – still runs alongside the Upper Forge Pool.

The Forge or *Upper Timlet Bridge* – a road still runs direct to the Bell Tong Norton, where *the Cross* still stands – minus the sacred sign and figure.

Will. Colemore Esq. – probably owner or tenant of Shackerley.

Ffitchherbot Esq. – one of the Boscobel family.

The Keeper's Meadows – names still retained near Tong Park House.

"Marle pits" – the ancient De Hugefort deed is thus translated:*And that they (The monks) may have all liberty and free common in woods, in plains, in highways, in paths, in waters, in mills, in heaths, in turbaries [places where peat is dug], in quarries, in fisheries, in marl pits [where calcareous clay for fertiliser is dug], and in all other places, and easements [the right of a landowner to make use of his neighbour's land e.g. to cross it to reach his own property] to the aforesaid Manor of Tonge, belonging, and that they may take marl at their pleaure to marl their land.*

1719. One of the **bells** bears the inscription "Peace and good Neighbourhood A. R. 1719." The initials are those of Abraham Rudhall, the famous bell-founder of Gloucester, who in the next year re-cast the Big bell of Sir Henry Vernon.

A bond dated July 1st 1719 (bearing the signatures of Richard Pendrill, and the mark of ffrancis Pendrill) is among the church papers to this effect "Whereas Mary Yates, late of Brewood in the county of Stafford, singlewoman, hath some time agoe been delivered of a ffemale Bastard child in the Parish of Tonge, which may hereafter become chargeable to the same parish, and foreasmuch as one Humphry Pendrill (son of ffrances Pendrill of Essington in the county of Stafford, widow) was adjudged to be the ffather of the said bastard child, therefore the above mentioned ffrances Pendrill, and Richard Pendrill, of Essington in the county of Stafford, yeoman, doe and shall from time to time and at all times hereafter fully and clearly acquitt, discharge, save harmless, & Indempnife Thomas Woodshaw & Thomas Paynton, churchwardens of the parish church of Tonge aforesaid, and also overseers of the poor of the said parish, and their successors for the time being as also all the Inhabitants & parishioners of the said parish from all expenses, damages & Incumberances whatsoever, which may at any time arise by reason of the Maintenance, Education, nourishing or bringing up of the said Bastard child.

Sealed and delivered in the presence of John Yorke. J. Cowper."

The child referred to in the above is probably the one entered in the Tong Register

"1716, April 3. Mary, daughter of Mary Yates, a vagabond, baptized."

And in the bond of Jan. 6, 1714-5.

1720 The following Bill for re-casting the great bell is endorsed by the late Archdeacon Lloyd (whose representative sent it to the Vicar of Tong). "Copy of the original Bill for Tong big bell, given to me by Richard Duncalfe, of Lilleshall for the Shrewsbury Museum, April 1849. Duncalfe's ancestors had been ch'wardens of Tong."

	£	s	d
1720 Mr. Tho: Woodshaw & Mr. Tho: Painton churchwardens of ye Parish of Tong are debtors to Abr: Rudhall jun., the 30 of July 1720 for casting 41c – 00qr - 15li of old mettle which I recd. in May last past, ye sum of forty pounds	40	00	00
Ffor 05c- 03qr- 14li of new mettle at fourteen pence per pound yt comes to	38	07	08
ffor ye mettle being four pounds weight allowed to each hundredweight for what ye old mettle weighed at fourteen pence per pound comes to	09	11	04
pd. for new working ye clapper	01	09	00
pd. for ye balding ye pins, staples etc.	00	05	00
In all fact	89	13	00

The incorrect inscription put on it (see 1636) at this re-casting is "Quam perduellionum rabie fractam sumptibus parochiae refudit Abr. Rudhall. Glocest: anno 1720[63]. L. Pietier, Min., T. Woodshaw, T. Peynton, oedituis."

1721. In this year a certain Thomas Burton made a survey of the Lordship of Tong, and gave the following report.

Neat acres	2376 ac.	0 roods	34 poles.
Lord Gower and Freeholders	634	1	28
Highways and Commons	356	1	6

The rest of this list is covered by the following printed notice

1722, Mar. 25	*William, s. of John Horton and Elizabeth*	*Bap.*
1722, April 11	*Richard Blackmore*	*Bur.*
1722, April 18	*Eliz: Sutton, of Norton*	*Bur.*
1722, April 28	*Anne Cowley*	*Bur.*
1722, April 28	*James Barnsley*	*Bur.*

The same day these two children were buryed, there was another dead in this Parish, ye **Small Pox** *then raging in it in a very mortal manner.*

---

[63] [Abraham Rudhall of Gloucester recast this bell, which had been broken in the madness of the Civil War, at parish expense/subscription in the year 1720.]

1722, *April 29*	*Sarah Horton*	*Bur.*
1722, *May 1*	*Anne Mason*	*Bur.*
1722, *May 4*	*Thomas Paynton*	*Bur.*
1722, *May 14*	*Thomas Swan*	*Bur.*
1722, *June 24*	*John Price, sen.*	*Bur.*
1722, *July 6*	*Joseph Ansel*	*Bur.*

The Vicar, The Vicarage, The Almshouses and the School

1725. On August 14, in this year a Deed was drawn up between the Most noble Evelyn, Duke of Kingston, Knight of the most noble order of the Garter, of the 1st part, Lewis Pietier, clerk, Minister or Curate of Tong, of the 2nd part, Peniston Lamb, of Lincoln's Inn, co. Middlesex, gentleman, Thomas Cromp, of Tong Castle, co. Salop, gentleman, Walter Stubbs, of Beckbury, co. Salop, gentleman, Richard Whiston, of Kilsall, co. Salop, gentleman, and Geoffrey Tildesley, of Tong, co. Salop, gentleman, of the 3rd part, and Sir Humphry Briggs of Haughton, co. Salop, Baronet, Thomas Jobber of Aston, co. Salop, Esquire, and Thomas Wood of Albrighton, co. Salop, clerk, of the 4th part. After reciting the above quoted deed of Gervas, Lord Pierrepont, of 1697, it goes on to say that Gervas, Lord Pierrepont, died in 1715, that by his death all his property came to Evelyn, Duke of Kingston, that Sir Humphry Briggs, the father, Thomas Jobber, the father, William Scott, Thomas Hatton, and Robert Moreton were dead, that the castle at Tong had been for a long time uninhabited, and the Parke, called Tong Park, disparked and enclosed, and that there was no prospect that the said castle would ever for the future be the residence of the said Duke of Kingston, or his family.[64] But the Duke of Kingston, being desirous that the settlements made by Lord Pierrepont in 1697 should be supported, has at his own charge, and upon his own freehold erected and built with brick a strong handsome and convenient house in Tong, of 4 rooms on a floor with a room for a library, and a stable, hayloft, brewhouse and other conveniences, for the

---

[64] Sir Humphrey Brigges died Jan 31, 1699, aged 41; the Rev. William Scott, Vicar of Albrighton 1688-1700, was buried at Albrighton Feb 5, 1700; Thomas Hatton was buried at Tong Oct 9, 1703.

habitation of the minister or curate of Tong, with the garden, orchard and other appertinances, for the use and benefit of the minister to be settled upon him and his successors for ever; and the Duke has also caused a catalogue to be made of all the books, being the same that were remaining with Lord Pierrepont at the time of his death, which has been signed by the said Duke and Lewis Pietier the present minister of Tong, and has delivered the books to the said minister for the use of himself and his successors. Therefore the covenants entered into by Lord Pierrepont for the minister's enjoying a room in the castle, and the use of the books, and library and the stable, and hayloft, and the privilege of grazing his horse in Tong Park are become unnecessary or cannot be performed. And whereas the common fields within the parish of Tong have since 1697 been enclosed and converted into pasture ground, and the revenue arising from the small tithes is greatly diminished, the same producing on an average, not above £12 per ann. the annuity of £30 shall be settled on the said minister and his successors for ever instead of the said tithes. It is therefore declared that the said trustees shall pay the several annuities of £30; £30; £14 and £6, making the yearly sum of £80, to Lewis Peitier, curate of Tong and his successors in the said parish at the said house built by the Duke of Kingston, by half yearly payments.

 As for the yearly rent of £10 to be employed in buying flax and hemp to be manufactured into cloth by the poor and the profit and produce to be employed in placing and binding out as apprentices such of the poor children of Tong whose parents shall not be thought able to maintain them, no children shall be apprenticed unless the minister shall approve. Further for providing a habitation for the curate of Tong and his successors, the Duke of Kingston has lately built that messuage or tenement situate standing and being in Tong, and now grants the soil and seite of the same, fronting East towards and abutting on the street or way leading from Tong to Dunnington, and on the West towards a footpath or way leading from the church at Tong to Tong Castle, and on the North towards a house and garden of the said Duke of Kingston now in possession of Robert Scholey, and on the <u>South</u> to a meadow called Hell Meadow, and the stable, hayloft, brewhouse and all other outhouses, erections and buildings lately built by the said Duke of Kingston upon the said site, and all that garden and orchard lying continuous to the said tenement, in Tong and all the rooms, chambers, cellars, solars, lights, easements, walls, hedges, fences, ditches, ways, waters, watercourses belonging to the said site. And for the better and more effectual establishing and promoting the general charity, and for providing an habitation for the six poor widows to be placed in the almshouses, the Duke of Kingston grants all that almshouse or ancient chapel situated in Tong, endowed with the annuity of £12, and also the garden or gardens belonging to the same to be held by the six poor widows, provided always, as any vacancy shall happen, they be nominated by the Lord or Owner of the manor of Tong as long as it shall be in the family of the Duke of Kingston, and then afterwards by the trustees of the said almshouse for the time being, or the major part of them. And whereas Evelyn, Duke of Kingston, and Gervas, Lord Pierrepont and their ancestors, Lords of the Manor of Tong for the time being have for a great many years last past paid £4 a year towards maintaining a schoolmaster employed to teach the poor children of the parish to read, and have provided a schoolhouse for him in Tong, but there has yet been no settlement or assurance of the said schoolhouse or annual stipend of £4 a year for the benefit of the said schoolmaster, the Duke of Kingston hereby grants all that messuage or tenement situate standing and being near the west end of the churchyard in Tong, now used and occupied as a schoolhouse, and all ways, passages, yards and privileges, to be used and employed as a school for the teaching of 10 poor boys within the parish of Tong to read, and for the instructing them in the Principles of the Christian Religion according to the doctrine of the Church of England as by law established and for a habitation for the schoolmaster for ever, provided that the schoolmaster of the school shall, from time to time, as any vacancy shall happen, be nominated by the Lord or Owner of the Manor of Tong so long as it shall be in the family of the Duke of Kingston, and afterwards by the trustees for the time being or the greater part of them. And further for the better support of the said school the Duke of Kingston doth grant and confirm an annuity or yearly rent charge of £4 stirling out of all lands being within the manor and parish of Tong by half yearly payments. Finally the deed declares that when the trustees shall be reduced to the number of two, they shall elect 5 other sufficient, proper, respectable and neighbouring persons to be trustees of, for, and concerning the above annuities, charges and charities.

The original catalogue of the minister's library is in the church chest. On the outside of the parchment is written
"Catalogue of Tong Library given by Lord Pierrepont and Rev. Mr. Pietier" (in handwriting of Rev. T. Hall).
"Given to me Jan. 28 1817 by Mr. J. Glover of Burlington. G.Durant" (in handwriting of Mr. Durant).
"Restored to the vicar of Tong, August 13th, 1895, by Oswald Mangin Holden, M.A., B.C.L., clerk, Vicar of Gailey cum Hatherton, Staffs." (in handwriting of Rev. J. H. Courtney-Clarke.)[65]
It consists of three leaves of parchment, two containing a list of the books given by Lord Pierrepont, in the handwriting of Rev. Lewis Pietier, the third those given by Mr. Pietier in the handwriting of Rev. T. Hall.
Lord Pierrepont gave 359 books, which were divided into "5 presses." The catalogue begins
In ye first Press

1	Conciliorum pars prima	19vol s	Parisiis 1644
2	A rational illustration for ye book of common prayer by Charles Wheatley	1 vol	London 1720

---

[65] "It was presented to Mr. Holden by Miss Durant in token of her appreciation of his kindness to her nephew who lived and died at Gailey." (Note by Mr. Clarke in his church register).

3   Sebaltiani Barradii comen-
    taria in concordiam et his-
    toriam Evangelicam   3 vols   Moguntiae 1618

The third sheet is entitled "A catalogue of the books belonging to the late Reverend Mr. Lewis Peitier, curate of Tong, devised by his last will bearing date August 31, 1742 to the library belonging to the curacy of Tong to make part of it for ever." And at the bottom of the list is written "N.B. The Rev. Mr. Peitier died 2nd August 1745, and this catalogue (as well as the catalogue of the library given by the late Lord Pierrepont to the curate of Tong and his successors contained on 2 other sheets of parchment hereto annext) was examined and found right this 8th day of August 1745 [signed] Sam. Shering. Thomas Hall."

There are many French, Italian and classical books among the 90 volumes given by Mr. Peitier.

Beriah Botfield, Esq. F.R.S., F.S.A., M.P. published "A catalogue of the Minister's Library in the Collegiate Church of Tong in Shropshire," a copy of which the Rev. J. H. Courtney-Clarke, Vicar 1891-96, had bound with blank pages at the end for additions, and presented to the church in 1891.
The report of the Charity Commissioners dated Jan 15, 1820 (page 260) says "Some additions are occasionally made to it by Mr. Durant, but it does not seem to have been heretofore sufficiently secure against losses, a diminution having been found in March 1812, of 59 volumes from the no. of 554 comprised in the catalogue." Mr. Botfield only describes 409 volumes and says, "The books have retained their original bindings of calf; but the set of Councils may be easily distinguished by its vellum covering. The bibliographer will look in vain for any work of surpassing interest." The binding however of the copy of *Johannes de Sancto Geminiano, Venetiis, 1499, is worth notice, for it is stamped with the Tudor Rose, and the Pomegranate, surmounted by a crown, the badge of Catherine of Aragon, whose*

first husband was Prince Arthur of Wales when Sir Henry Vernon of Tong was Governor and who herself resided some time at Ludlow Castle.

In 1725 according to a Tract in the British Museum **the Lizard Forge** made at that time and had made annually in the past 140 tons of iron – **Norton Forge** had made and did make 140 tons.

1727. On the loose paper containing notices of 1696, and 1701, is a third entry as follows, but no sum is mentioned.
"1727 Paid for new pales to Church yd."

"Sept 20 John, s. of George Baddely and Sarah baptized."
This boy afterwards became somewhat well known, for according to Shaw's Staffordshire, under Smethwick, "**Mr. John Baddely**, born at Tong, co. Salop in 1727, after receiving a common school education, was put to work by his father and followed for some years the humble calling of a blacksmith, but being averse to the shoeing of horses, and feeling himself, as he thought, capable of a better employment, at the age of 18 he quitted his father's business and commenced watch and clock making, an undertaking in which by dint of superior talents and great integrity he soon established himself and acquired the degree of reputation which he still continues to enjoy. About the year 1752 (having received some very good instruction in the principles of mechanics) he turned his attention to optics and constructed reflecting telescopes of uncommon excellence. In his specula the parabolic was preferred to the usual spherical figure, from which he conceives material advantages in point of light and distinctness are obtained. His superiority as a clockmaker will be told for some ages to come by the numerous domestic and turret clocks substantially constructed by him in every part of the county within many miles of Albrighton where he has long resided."
The Albrighton Register records his burial in 1804
"Jan. 30. John Baddely, gent., aged 76."

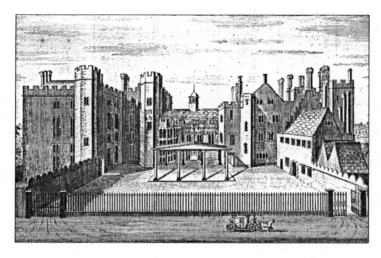

This view of Tong castle drawn by Buck in 1731 shows the castle before George Durant altered it.

1731. Buck's view of the East side of the Castle built by Sir Henry Vernon circa 1500, is dated 1731. John Leland in his Itinerary writing about 1540, when speaking of Tong says "There was an olde Castel of stone caullid Tunge Castle. Syr Henry Vernun a late daies made it new al of Bricke."

At the Castle was in my time a M.S. entitled on the cover "Trust Estates. Mr. Richard Whiston's Account for One Year Ending Lady Day 1731, and 1732," of which the following is a transcript.

[the following accounts, 1728-1731, not printed in Vol 1, come from Auden's first Notebook]

Manor of Tong and Tong Norton, Com. Salop

An account adjusted with Mr. Richard Whiston for Rents and Profits of the Estate of the most Noble Evelyn, Duke of Kingston there, for one year ending atLady Day 1731.

1730 Charges

Arrears 1728

Jeffry Tildesley in arrear for part of half a
year's rent due Lady Day, 1728   9   7   6

Rental 1730
The Rents for the Half Year due Michael-
mas, 1730, £511.4.5½.
The Rents for the Half Year due Lady
Day, 1731, £511.3.11½   1022   8   5

Casual Profits
Casual Profit
The Great Tythes for the year 1730, as per
Acct. £85.10. 6½
The Small Tythes for the year 1730, as per
Acct. £10.10.11
Recd. a Herriot due on the death of Tho-
mas Pemberton, £4.0.0.
Recd.of the Lady Bradford for 1500 of
Tyle at 15s. £1.2.6.   101   3   11½

1730 Discharge
Court Charges and Woodman's Fee
Charges of the court held for the Manor of
Tong 26 Nov. 1730   17s 0d.
Mr. Stubb's Fee for keeping the same
£1.
To John Cotton for care of the Woods one
year to Lady Day 1731 £2.   3   17   0
Outpayments etc.
To the King's Audit per Mr. Lucas, one
year's Fee Farm Rent, (Tenths) for Landes
in Tong, parcel of Vernon's Chantry, due
at Michaelmas, 1730 -   3s.10d. and acq.
10d; Messenger 1s.   5   8
To Sir Theophilus Bidolph, as Lord of the
Manor at Lapley, one years Rent, (Tenths)
out of Tong College, due at Michaelmas
1730, 15s. messenger 6d.   15   6
Allowed several payments chargeable on

the Manor of Tong by his late Grace's settlement of 24 Aug. 1725, viz.

To the Rev. Mr. Peitier, Minister (or Curate) of Tong, half a year's payment due Michaelmas 1730	40	0	0
To him more the Half Year due Lady Day 1731	40	0	0
To the Minister, Churchwardens and Overseers of the Poor of the Parish of Tong, half a year's payment for the six widdows in the Almshouse there, due Michaelmas 1730	6	0	0
To them more to buy Staffordshire wool to make into cloth for the said widdows and other Poor	6	0	0
To them more to buy Hemp and Flax to be made into Cloth and sold, and the produce applied in placing out Poor children apprentice	5	0	0
To the said Trustees, the Three last Sums to Lady Day 1731	17	0	0
To the Schoolmaster of Tong for Teaching 10 boys, one year to Lady Day 1731	4	0	0
To the Rev. Mr. Peitier half a year's annuity due at Michaelmas 1730; secured to him out of Hubbald Farm, by Deed of 24 Aug. 1725	10	0	0
To him for more for the half Year due Lady Day 1731	10	0	0
TOTAL	139	1	2

Taxes and Parish Dues

Allowed the 4 Quarterly Payments of Land Tax at 2s. per £ for 1730 for the Castle, Gardens, Demesnes, Park Lands, the Mill, Tythes and Wood-land (each Qr. year £1.19.10.)	7	19	4
Allowed 3 Lewns and ½ to the church of Tong for 1730 for the same	2	0	11
Allowed 4 Lewns to the Poor there for 1730 for Do.	2	11	4
Allowed the Constable's lewn there for 1730 for Do.		12	10
Allowed Thomas Pemberton's wid. (according to his lease) half Land Tax for 1730, and half lewns to the Church, Poor, and Constable of Tong for 1730.		14	8
TOTAL	13	19	1

Repairs

To John Blakemore for mending Rails, Pails, Gates etc at the Park Meadow, Conygres and Coppices' Gates		8	9
To the Glazier for mending the Chancel Windows		10	9
To Thomas Jones for making 21,000 of Brick at 10s; 28,800 of Plain Tyle at 1s.6d.; and for levelling the ground to work on as per bill	32	15	9
Allowed Saml. Bott's Execrs. for hedging at the Flores and for removing a building as per bill	1	11	0
TOTAL	35	6	3

Planting etc.

To several Persons for Planting Trees out of the Colledge Nursery into several parts of the Lordship, as per bill	3	11	0
More for weeding Quick at the Park Meadow		11	9
To several Persons for Hedging at the Woods as per bill	1	6	8
TOTAL	5	9	5

Charges and improvements

Allowed Watkin Williams Wynne, Esq. for Supplying the Castle with water one year to Lady Day 1731, according to the agreement in his Article for the Castle etc. till the Engine that used to supply the same be repaired	10	0	0
Allowed Geo. Holmes one year's rent for an acre of land used for a Brick Kiln to Lady Day 1731		7	0
Allowed the Widow Yates the 4th and 5th year's allowance at 19s. per ann. for clearing Rough Ground to Lady Day 1731	1	18	0
TOTAL	12	5	0

Arrears 1728

Jeffry Tildesley in arrear for part of half a year's rent due Lady Day 1728	9	7	6

Expenses of the House and Gardens

Allowed one year's Window Tax for the Castle	1	10	0
Allowed also one year's wages to the Clark at Tong to Easter 1730		5	0
To John Fox, the Gardiner, according to			

an agreement with his late Grace, half a year's payment for taking care of the gardens and all expenses of keeping the same to Mich. 1730	25	0	0
To him more for his wife's taking care of the House and Furniture to the same time	5	0	0
To them more on same acct. half a year to Lady Day 1731	30	0	0
To John Fox, a small bill for necessaries for the House		6	8
To Thomas Daynte for 9 stacks of Coals and Expenses of fetching the same in July 1730	2	18	2
To Mr. Woodman, a bill for Fruit Trees sent from London		7	8
TOTAL	65	7	6

Repairs

To Thomas Pyat, the Mason, for work done at the Castle etc. to Feb. 18 1730		16	0
To Geo. Baddeley, the Smith, for work done there, per bill		6	3
To William Blakemore and Edward Rudge for straw and for Thatching the College Barn as per bill	2	17	6
Paid for 3 Load of Lyme		4	6
TOTAL	4	4	3

Receiver's Salary and Allowances

Allowed the Accountant one year's Salary to Lady Day 1731	30	0	0
To him more for Postage of Letters to 1 Oct. 1731 as per bill	1	0	10
Also for Fetching and Carrying of letters one year to same time	1	6	0

Allowed him also what he paid for Return of Money to London	1	6	10
Also what he paid the Master in Chancery (extra) for taking his affidavit to his Acct. for 1729		5	0
Allowed him also for Stationary Ware as usual		11	6
Also the expenses of his Journey to Thoresby in Nov. 1730, to Pass his Accts. for 1729	2	17	6
TOTAL	37	7	8

Ready Money Payments to the Executors
1730

Feb 13	*Paid them per Bill on Hollis & Co.*	62	0	0
Feb 19	*Paid them more per Do.*	60	0	0
Mar 13	*Paid them more per Do.*	62	0	0
1731				
April 5	*Paid them more per Do.*	60	0	0
April 23	*Paid them more per Do.*	62	0	0
May 28	*Paid them more per Do.*	67	0	0
July 23	*Paid them more per Bill on Olly.*	88	4	0
Aug 5	*Paid them more per bill on Cal-cot*	130	0	0
Oct 29	*Paid them more per bill on Hollis*	100	0	0
	Paid them more per Do.	83	9	9
Dec 7	*Paid them more per Cash Note*	32	1	3½
	TOTAL	806	15	0½

I have compared this account with the Rentalls and with the former Year's Book and I have examined into the Casual Profits herein charged and into the several Articles of the Discharge, and do not find any error therein. Witness my hand this 10th Day of Dec. 1731.   (Signed) Tho: Cromp.

Com. Salop. Manor of Tong and Tong Norton.
An Account Adjusted with Mr. Richard Whiston for the Rents and Profits of this Estate (being an Estate in Fee Simple) of the late Duke of Kingston for one year, ending at Lady Day 1732.

	£	s	d
Arrears 1728			
Jeffrey Tildesley in arrear for part of half a year's Rent due at Lady Day 1728	9	7	6
Rental			
The Rents for the half year due at Michaelmas 1731	504	14	5½
The Rents for the half year due at Lady day 1732	503	18	11½
TOTAL	1,008	13	5
Casual Profit			
The Great Tythes for the year 1731 as per Agreement	80	19	10
The Small Tythes for the year 1731 as per Account	15	13	8
Recd. for the Ley of Salter's Conygrees and Horse Rail Meadows, while they were in hand from Lady Day 1731 to Michaelmas 1731	7	17	4
TOTAL	104	10	10
Court Charges, Gamekeeper and Woodman Fee			
Charges of the Court held 21 October 1731		17	0
Mr.Stubb's Fee for keeping the same	1	0	0
To John Cotton, the Game Keeper, one year's Salary to Lady Day 1732	2	0	0
To J. Cooper and J. Plant for Fencing the Woods one year to Do.	2	0	0
TOTAL	5	17	0

To the King's Audit per Mr. Lucas one year's Fee farm Rent (Tenths) for Land in Tong, Parcel of Vernon's Chantry, to Mich. 1731, 3s. 10d.; acq. 10d.; Messenger 1s.		5	8
To Sir Theophilus Bidolph as Lord of the Manor of Lapley one year's Rent (Tenths), out of Tong College, due at Michaelmas 1731, 15s. messenger 6d.		15	6
Allowed several Payments chargeable on the manor of Tong by his late Grace's settlement of 24 August 1725, viz :-			
To the Rev. Mr. Peitier, Minister (or Curate) of Tong half a year's Payment due at Michaelmas 1731	40	0	0
To him more the half year due at Lady Day 1732	40	0	0
To the Minister, Churchwardens, and Overseers of the Poor of the Parish of Tong half a year's Payment for the 6 widdowes in the Almshouse there due at Michaelmas 1731	6	0	0
To them more to buy Hemp and Flax to make into Cloth and sold, and the produce thereof applied in placing out Poor Children apprentice	5	0	0
To them more to buy Staffordshire wool to make into cloth for the said widdows and other Poor	6	0	0
To the said Trustees the last three mentioned sums to Lady Day 1732	17	0	0
To the Schoolmaster of Tong for Teaching 10 boys one year to Do.	4	0	0
To the Rev. Mr. Peitier two half year's Annuity, secured to him out of Hubbal Farm by Deed of 24 August 1725, due at Lady Day 1732	20	0	0
TOTAL	139	1	2

Taxes and Parish Duties

	£	s	d
Allowed the 4 Quarterly Payments of Land Tax at 2s. per £ for 1731 for the Castle, Gardens, Desmesnes, Park Land, Mill, Tythes, Woodland each qr. £2.0.0.	8	8	0
Allowed Lewns to the Church of Tong for Do. for 1731		12	10
Allowed Lewns to the Poor of Tong for Do. for 1731	2	11	4
Allowed Lewns to the Constable of Tong for Do. for 1731		16	0½
Allowed Thomas Pemberton's heir (according to his lease) half Land Tax for 1731, and half Lewns to Church, Poor and Constable of Tong for 1731		15	4½
TOTAL	13	3	6½

Repairs of the Castle

	£	s	d
Paid John Blakemore for Cleaving 3,000 Heart Laths, and 1,900 Sap Laths, and some Carpenter's work at several places to 15 March 1731	3	9	11
Paid for Carriage of 4 Trees to Rive into Laths		10	0
Paid James Wedge for Carpenter's work to 28 March, 1732		16	6
Paid Thomas Pyat, the Mason, per Bill to 30 Oct 1731		18	6
Paid for mending the Chancel Windows in Dec 1731		4	3
Paid for 8 Horse Load of Lyme for Repairs 14 Oct 1731		12	0
Paid for Thatching at the College to 15 June 1731	6	0	3
Paid several Persons for work at the Conygres and Meadows after Mr. Williams left them & while they were in hand to Mich: 1731	3	4	2
TOTAL	15	15	7

Improvements

Allowed one year's rent for the Brick Kiln to Lady Day 1732		7	0
Paid John Fox, the Gardiner, a Bill for Labourer's work in planting Trees out of the Nursery about several parts of the Lordship.	3	0	8
TOTAL	3	7	8

Arrears

Jeffrey Tildesley in arrear for part of a half a Year's Rent at Lady Day 1728	9	7	6
Thomas Ore for the Knowle half a year to Lady Day 1732	7	0	0
More for half a years Chief Rent to same time		1	6
Anne Bolt a year to same time		8	0
Jos: Horton the same to same time		8	0
TOTAL	17	5	0

Expenses of Tong Castle and Gardens

Allowed one year's Window Tax for the Castle to Lady Day 1732	1	10	0
Allowed one year's Clarks Wages to Easter 1731		5	0
To John Fox, the Gardner, according to an Agreement with his late Grace, half a year's Payment for taking care of the Gardens and all expenses of keep the same to Michaelmas 1731	25	0	0
To him more for his wife's taking care of the Castle and Furniture to same time.	5	0	0
To them more the half year for Do. to Lady Day 1732	30	0	0
Paid for a Dozen of Candles for the use of the castle		7	0
Paid for Glasses and Earthen Ware	1	5	0

Paid for Stack of Coles, brot. by 12 Boon Teams in July 1731	3	16	5
Paid John Fox a bill for necessarys for the Use of the Castle.	1	6	1
Paid for Corn, Hay, Straw for the stables when Mr Cromp was at Tong in October 1731	1	9	6
Paid J. Baddeley for carriage of 257 Hhds of Water to the Castle from 30 March 1730 to 24 March 1731 at 3d per Hhd	3	4	3
Paid John Smith and others for Fishing the Hawkshead Pools		6	0
Paid Mr Woodman for Trees sent from London	1	18	0
TOTAL	75	7	3

Receiver's Salary and Allowances

Allowed the Accountant one year's Salary to Lady Day 1732	30	0	0
To him more a Bill for Post Letters to 16 March 1731		16	4
More for Carriage of Letters one year to Lady Day 1732	1	6	0
To him also his Usual Allowance for Stationery Ware to Do.		11	6
To him more what he paid a Master in Chancery for takeing an Affidavit to his Accts. For 1730.		5	0
Allowed him also what he paid for Returns of Money.	1	8	6
TOTAL	34	7	4

Money Payments to the Executors.

By a Bill on Hollis & Co.	82	0	0
By Do.	35	5	0
By 2 Bills on Calcot	145	11	0
By a Bill on Hollis & Co	50	0	0
By a Bill on Do.	38	0	0
By a Bill on Sells	74	0	0
By a Bill on Hollis & Co	70	0	0
By a Bill on Do.	150	0	0
By a Bill on Do.	80	0	0
TOTAL	724	16	0

I have perused this account and compared it with the Rental and with the former Year's Book and have examined into the Casual Profits herein charged and into the several Articles of the Discharge and do not find any error therein.
Witness my hand this ninth day of June 1733.
(Signed) Thos: Cromp

The payment of a Fee Farm rent for the Golden Chapel to the king is interesting. On the dissolution of the College of Tong, temp. Henry VIII, the whole of its possessions were granted to Sir Richard Manners for the sum of £486. 4s. 2d. This was confirmed to him by Edward VI in the 1st year of his reign to hold to him and his heirs of the king in capite by the service of the 40th part of a knight's fee and an annual rent of £5. 14s. 0½d, with a further annual rent of 12s 11d for Vernon's Chauntry in the Church of Tong.

*1733-4. Jan. 29. **Francis Taylor** of Stapleford, in the county of Lincoln, buried.*
He was buried at the West end of the North Aisle where his gravestone was discovered in 1889 during excavations for a warming apparatus bearing the following inscription. "In memory of Francis Taylor of Stapleford, Lincolnshire who departed this life at Tonge Castle, the 28th day of January 1733 aged 63." It was covered over again however.

1734. On May 30, a conveyance was drawn up between John Cotterill, the elder, of Albrighton, co. Salop, yeoman, and John Cotterill, the younger, son and heir of John Cotterill the elder, of the 1st part, Anne Bowdler of Madeley, co. Salop, spinster, of the 2nd, Lewis Pietier, Minister of Tong, co. Salop, Walter Clay of Hubbole, in the parish of Tong, and John Picken of Tong, Churchwardens of the parish and parish church of Tong, and Richard Whiston of Kilsall, co. Salop, gentleman, Richard Evans of Tong, yeoman, and Thomas Fox of Tong, yeoman, of the 3rd part. The sum of £100 had been given by the late Lady Harris for the use of the Poor of the parish of Tong, and a sum of £200 was since likewise given by the last will and testament of the late Lady Pierpont, and the sum of £100, was now the gift of the said Lewis Pietier, making a total of £400. This sum was, by this agreement, spent in the purchase of a messuage or tenement and divers lands in the parish of Albrighton called the "Dead Woman's Grave," or **Harriots Hayes**. The former name, according to tradition, comes from the fact that the spot where the two roads meet, is the burial place of a woman who hanged herself in a slipping of yarn.[66]

1734. On Dec. 13, new Charity Trustees were elected. The indenture is between Walter Stubbs and Richard Whiston of the 1st part; Lewis Pietier of the 2nd part; Sir Hugh Brigges, Baronet, Robert Aglionby Slaney, Esquire, Francis West, Doctor in Divinity, James Devey, and John Stubbs, gentlemen, of the 3rd part. By it, since Evelyn, Duke of Kingston, and Sir Humphry Brigges, Thomas Jobber the son, and Thomas Wood, three of the old trustees were dead, Walter Stubbs and Richard Whiston the survivors, chose the above 5 new ones.[67]

1735. April 21. William Clay, son of Walter Clay and Margaret his

---

[66] S.A.S.T. Vol XI 2nd series
[67] The Duke of Kingston died March 5, 1726, aged 60; Thomas Wood, Vicar of Albrighton 1701-1725, died Sept. 25, 1725.

wife buried.
　　April 29. John Felews, a soldier, buried.

At the restoration in 1892, a slab was found near the west door bearing the inscription "Here lieth the Body of William Clay, son of Walter and Margaret Clay who Departed this Life April ye 18th 1735 aged 18 years."

1738. Dec. 11. *"The Honourable Henry Willoughby Esq. buried. An Affidavit not being received on the nineteenth of December, Notice thereof was given to a Churchwarden and Overseer the same day."*

The Hon. Henry Willoughby was the youngest son of Lord Middleton, and was tenant of Tong Castle where he died Dec. 3, 1738 aged 33. He was buried in a vault in the centre of the chancel between the Vestry and the Priest's Door, and his memorial slab of black marble is much worn by the feet of those who have walked over it. On it however the Middleton arms are clear viz: Quarterly 1st and 4th or fretty az.; 1st 2nd and 3rd or, on two bars gu., three water-bougets arg. two and one, crest, bust of a man, couped at the shoulders, affronté, ducally, crowned. Supporters - Dexter, a grey friar in his habit; Sinister a savage with a club in his exterior hand, each supporter holding a banner ensigned with an owl. Motto Veritate sans peur[68].

The inscription is much rubbed but "the following lines" can be with difficulty made out, they are found in the Rev. R. G. Lawrence's M.S.

　　　　His noble soul and truly generous mind,
　　　　In acts of goodness both were unconfined;
　　　　His charity was free and private too
　　　　His proper objects felt but known to few.
　　　　His hospitality the poor did share,
　　　　Relieved the widow, dried the orphans tear;
　　　　Pride with its lures and vain attempting art,
　　　　Hateful to sight, was absent from his heart
　　　　A friend he was most worthy and sincere
　　　　There did the lustre of the friend appear,

---

[68] *[Fearlessly by truth]*

And as his merits justly claimed a name
Inscribed in annals of immortal fame
In his just praise to latest times be it said
That all who living knew him mourned him dead.

1739. Oct. 24 **Thomas Poole,** *officer of Excise buried.* His tombstone was discovered in the North Aisle in 1892 bearing the inscription "Here lieth the Body of Thomas Poole who departed this life Oct. the 21 ano. 1739 aged 51". It has now been placed with those of W. Clay (1735) and W. Scott (1694) at the West end of the North Aisle.

A most interesting map, a copy of which was presented to the Vicar of Tong in 1900 by H. G. Duncalfe Esq. of Wolverhampton is inscribed "A Map of the Manor of Tong and Tong Norton in the County of Salop for ye Most Noble Evelyn Duke of Kingston, Knight of the Most Hon. Order of ye Garter, renewed in ye Yeare 1739 by S. Reynolds." (The Duke had died March 5, 1726.)

1743. At the Jan Sessions (Quarter) A presentment was made by the parish constable against John Carpenter the younger, Tong, "for not sending his Parish Apprentice to the Ch of England, but sending him, or rather compelling him to go to the Popish religion." (cf 1672)

1747. The only man eligible to serve on a Jury in Tong in 1747 was John Roden, gent., of Ruckley.

1752. A bond dated March 20, 1752 bears the signature of "**William Howe**, of ye Parish of Tonge, in ye County of Salop, gentleman." He was the grandson of William Pendrill of Boscobel by "Dame" Joan his wife, his mother being Mary Pendrill, their daughter, who had married Thomas How. He is described in Hughes' Boscobel (p. 366-379) as "William Howe of Kiddermore Green, commonly styled Major Howe," but this is probably confusing him with the Major William Howe, ancestor of the Bromley Baronets, who was an illegitimate grandson of Prince Rupert (see Burke's Peerage "Bromley Bart.").

1756. In the July of this year (July 26) was born at Tong Castle **Mary Ann Smythe,** the youngest daughter of Walter Smythe, the second son of Sir John Smythe, of Acton Burnell Park, Salop. According to Mr. H. F. J. Vaughan[69], she was born in the Red Room at the Castle, having arrived somewhat unexpectedly during a visit of her parents. In 1775, at the age of 19, she married Edward Weld, of Lulworth Castle, Dorset. He died towards the end of the year, and in 1778 she married Thomas **Fitzherbert,** of Swynnerton, Staffordshire, who died in 1781. Lastly on Dec. 21, 1785, **she was united to the Prince of Wales,** (afterwards George IV), by a Protestant clergyman in the presence of her uncle, Henry Errington, and her brother John. She died at Brighton March 29, 1837 aged 81. Eleanor Woolley used to say that Mrs. Fitzherbert's father was in jeopardy at Tong Castle for something akin to treason having assisted some traitor to escape, and that the king's servants came to arrest him, thus bringing about her rather hasty birth. Eleanor Woolley's mother was wet nurse to the infant girl.
Cf. Cole "Mr. Carrington Smith, a R. C. gentleman, tenant of Tong Castle." (see also 1763).
Mary Ann Smyth was born at Tong Castle, the midwife being Margaret Woolley, wife of John Woolley. The latter was a Holliar and was married at Tong Sept. 26, 1734 and was buried at Tong April 24, 1802 aged 98. She also acted as wet-nurse to the infant girl, her own son, James, having been born in 1755. Margaret Woolley's grandson was a celebrated clock-maker who died in Dec. 1856, aged 79, and who corroborated the above, as did Eleanor, daughter of Margaret Woolley.

1757. Under the date July 28 1757 **Mr. William Cole, the Antiquary**, makes this note (Add. M.S. 5830 Brit. Mus.):-

---

[69] S. A. S. T. pt I, vol ix (Oct 1885) p. 60 cf B. G. Sept 6, 1906.

Tong Church stands by the great road from London to Chester. It is of the red stone of the country. It is in remarkable good repair even on the outside, as this sort of stone is apt to moulder and look ruinous by the weather. The College is on the south side of the Churchyard and is quite compleat, being a square, and has only changed its leaden roof for a thatched one, the building being of stone and in good repair. At the west end of the Churchyard and along the street stands some very old Almshouses, also in good repair, and seems to have a chapel of its own…. Camden observes that the inhabitants boast of nothing more than of a Great Bell famous in these parts for its Bigness, but I think they have more to boast of than most country places in having a noble Castle now rented of the Duke of Kingston by Mr. Carrington-Smith, a Roman Catholic gentleman of ancient family; in having a very handsome church fuller of Monuments of Antiquity than any I ever saw for its capacity; and for having its original College and Hospital still standing and in good repair, notwithstanding the general Havock and Destruction of such sort of Buildings throughout the kingdom….. In the Body and Nave of the Church lie 4 or 5 Altar Tombs of Marble or Alabaster with figures of Men and their wives on them, all in exceeding good Preservation…..but I had so little time to spare, it striking 7 o'clock during my continuence in the Church, and I had to go about 7 miles to Newport that evening that I could not gratify my desire in taking a particular account of these curious old Tombs; round the neck of one of these knights I observed a fresh garland of flowers and was informed that an Estate was held by the Tenure of putting such a Chaplet every year about this time on the said Tomb.

In the Chancel …one monstrous large Canopy Tomb stands jostling the Altar and before it, placed there, as I should guess by the form of it, for I only put these few notes down by Memory 3 weeks and more after my view of them, in the indecent reign of Queen Elizabeth…..These in the Chancel being of more Modern date and awkward Form struck not my fancy like those in the Body of the Church.....Time was so pressing, yet I could not resist the Temptation of one which lies in the very midst of the neat Chapel, out of regard to beloved Alma Mater, and was only half concerned that I could not stay long enough to take a sketch of it, as on the grey marble was the figure of a Priest shorn and in his proper Master of Arts habit as worn at that time which was different from what it is at present, being more like a Batchelor of Arts with large open sleeves; over his head was the cup and wafer, and at the four corners his coat of arms viz: at two corners single for Vernon, viz fretty; and at the 2 others Vernon and five others among which I thought I observed one of Trumpington, with two trumpets reversed etc. At his feet was this inscription all in brass.

Orate specialiter pro Aia Arthuri Vernon In Artibus Magri Universitatis Cantibrigie qui obiit XV Die Augusti Ano. Dni MCCCCCXVII cuius Aie p'picietur Deus[70].

On the floor and just at the foot of Arthur Vernon's gravestone and on the only step in the Chapel lies the old Altar stone as Part of the Pavement of it. In a sort of Vestry close to the Chancel among other old lumber is the very same organ case and Bellows belonging to it which was in use before the dissolution of the College, a piece of antiquity hardly to be parallelled in the whole kingdom. The Organ was small but the case of oak is very neat, and of a pretty Gothic Fashion. The door of this "sort of vestry close to the chancel" is remarkable for "three peculiar holes the use of which it is difficult to explain"! Possibly they were made in order that the priest might see the High Altar.

---

[70] [Pray especially for the soul of Arthur Vernon, Master of Arts in the University of Cambridge, who died the 15th day of August 1517. May God have mercy on his soul.]

Sir Arthur Vernon, priest, son of Sir Henry Vernon. This picture of his brass is taken from Griffiths: A History of Tong and Boscobel. A significant and unusual bust of Sir Arthur is on the west wall of the Golden Chapel in Tong Church.

By the original rules of the college of 1410 "a lamp was to be kept always burning before the High Altar", and the present vestry may have been built for the use of the priests, who, each in their turn, had the duty to perform of keeping this lamp alight. But much more likely for the convenience of those censering the High Altar.

The position of the large canopy tomb, as described by Mr. Cole, is an interesting proof that when it was erected "the Eastward Position" was the rule at Tong, as with this monument in its place over the Stanley vault it would have been impossible to take the "North Side" in the sense of North End. Mr. Street, in his plans for the restoration, contemplated moving it back to its old site within the altar rails. It was removed to where it at present stands, according to Mr. Lawrence's M.S. about 1805.[71]

1758. Oct. 5. Daniel Higgs, gentleman buried.
His monument is a brass over the door into the Golden Chapel bearing the inscription:- "Near this place is interred the Body of Daniel Higgs, gent, Steward to his Grace of Kingston, who departed this life Oct. 1. 1758 in the 60th year of his age. Few so Honest, None more so."
There is also opposite it an alabaster tablet with the words:- "Near this place lieth the body of Maria Higgs, daughter of Daniel and Mary Higgs of Tong Castle, who departed this life the 9th of May, 1748 aged 19 months and ten days."

Tong Vicarage
1759. Terrier. Tonge in Comit: Salop   September 1759.
A Terrier or Account of the buildings ground, and endowment belonging to the curacy in the above said parish in virtue of a settlement made by the Honourable Gervase, afterward Lord Pierrepont, October 23, 1697, and since with variations confirmed by His Grace the Duke of Kingston, August 14, 1725.
  1. An house of four rooms on a floor below with another

---

[71] Rev. D.H.S. Cranage, Churches of Shropshire, pt. 1. p. 44.

large room for the library belonging to it by the above settlement containing in all about four bays of building.

2. A brewhouse with a chamber and a stable with a loft containing in all two bays of building.
3. A pig sty with a fold and another little building adjoining to it, both of them made of bricks.
4. A place for coals surrounded with brick walls.
5. A courtyard, garden, and orchard lying all round the house and bounded on the east end by the street or way leading through Tonge to Kilsall, on the west end by a footpath or way from the Church to the Castle, on the north side by a way into a backside and a garden or orchard of the Duke of Kingston and on the south side by a meadow.
6. Fourscore pounds a year sterling, one half payable at Lady Day, and the other half at Michaelmas, for the payment of which the Lordship of Tonge stands engaged.

An Account of old Dues to the Minister

For a burial eightpence. For registering and churching eightpence. For an house and offerings fourpence. For a son or daughter one penny. For a single communicant two pence. For a wedding without a license half a crown. For a wedding with a license five shillings.

To the Clerk

For a tenement fourpence. For a cottage two pence. At a churching fourpence. At a wedding one shilling. For making a grave sixpence. For a burial twopence.

An account of other perpetual gifts

1. A schoolhouse with a garden adjacent to the same for the use of the schoolmaster.
2. A room over the college porch belonging to the Manufactury instead of the chamber above the school.
3. An Almshouse with gardens for six widows.
4. Twelve pounds a year to be distributed among the six widows in the Almshouse.
5. Twelve pounds a year to be laid out in Staffordshire wool

to be made into cloath for making gowns for the above said six widows, and the remainder of the cloath to be distributed among the poor of the parish.

6. Ten pounds a year for buying of hemp and flax to be made into cloth to be sold: and the yearly income thereof to be applied in placing out poor children apprentices.

The nomination of the above said schoolmaster and widows is to continue in ye Duke of Kingston's family, and afterwards to belong to the Minister and Trustees.

The management and disposal of the money and manufactury belongs to the

Minister and Churchwardens or the majority of them, the Minister being one.

An account of other gifts.

The Right Honourable the Lady Pierrepont's and the Lady Harris's gift; together with the Reverend Lewis Peitier's, are all laid out in Albrighton Parish.

The two pews on the north side[72], the pulpit and reading desk belong to the Minister.

Thomas Hall, Curate. William Barker, Churchwarden.

Examined 7th May, 1835 J. Mott, Jno. Hawarth, D: Regrs.

Shifnal, August 20, **1763**. Mrs. Davenport is at Davenport House fitting it up for Mr. Smith (cf Cole, 1757): he leaves Tong Castle at Michaelmas. If you go to Tong Norton there will never be a good neighbour for you but Coz: Brook.

(letter of Mrs. G. Appleby to Miss Judith Stubbs.)

Concerning this terrier and other papers in the chest, Mr. Lawrence enters under June 10, 1874 "About a year after I came to Tong, I had some old papers, two deeds and a terrier, relating to the Glebe of Tong placed in my hands by a descendant of a for-

---

[72] The Statutes and Ordinances of the College of Tong show that the Lady Chapel at Tong was on the north side of the church:- Dicatur missa de S. Maria in capella ex parte boreali dictae ecclesiae. (Dugdale's Monasticon Anglicanum vol.viii. p. 1408)

mer curate of Tong. The story respecting them is to this effect. When Mr. Durant possessed nearly the whole parish and was doing just as he liked at Tong, he appropriated a certain portion of the glebe during the non-residence of an absentee vicar. These papers and M.S.S. were placed in safe custody by the then curate as evidence of what was once church property, with the charge that when the descendant of this curate of Tong, knew a vicar of Tong who would go into the matter, the papers were to be delivered up to him; hence my possession of them." The two deeds are extracts from those of 1697 and 1725, and are headed "Extracts of Deeds at Tong Castle respecting the Stipend and Residence of the Curate of Tong, and various Charities, settled on the Estate of the late Duke of Kingston, taken by order of the Right Rev. Lord Bishop of Lichfield, January 28th, 1839, by J. Brooke, Vicar of Shifnal, and Rural Dean."

1763. On pp. 162, 163 of the **Gentleman's Magazine is an account of Tong** from which the following is extracted.

"Tong Castle is an old irregular edifice, built of stone except the east wing which, being demolished in the Civil wars, was rebuilt with brick in the same style of building with the rest. The Church was once collegiate. It consists of a nave, two side aisles, a cross aisle and a choir, in which there are still remaining eight stalls on each side. There is also a chantry on the south side of the church; and on the north side of the choir another detached building, now used as a vestry. At the east end of this chantry there is this inscription on the wall: "Pray for the soul of Sir Henry Vernon, Knight, and Dame Anne his wife, which Sir Henry in the year of our Lord 1515 made and founded this chapel and chantry, and the said Sir Henry departed the 13th day of April in the year above said, and of your charity for the soul of Sir Arthur Vernon, priest, son of the said Sir Henry, on whose souls the Lord have mercy. Amen."

At the west end of the chantry there is a bust of Sir Arthur Vernon, and on the floor his portrait in brass with the usual inscription of "Orate pro anima" etc. On the north side of the choir lie the figures of Sir Thomas Stanley and his lady on a table monument supported by pillars of marble, curiously gilt and carved with their arms. At each end is a pyramid of black marble, one of which at the head is thrown down. There are four marble figures on the top of the monument, but all broke. Under the table lies the image of Sir Edward Stanley, son to Sir Thomas.[73]

On the north side of the chancel there is a bust in the wall of a daughter in the Pierpoint family, but no epitaph.[74] The ancient college where the clergy lived is mostly demolished, and what remains is partly inhabited by some poor people, and partly converted into a stable. Tong is now a perpetual curacy, and the Duke of Kingston allows the minister £80 per annum. At the west end of the church there are almshouses, founded by some of the Harris family[75], for six poor widows, who have 40s., a shift and gown per annum. The lands produce great plenty of all sorts of grain, and the nature of the soil is dry and sandy."

A somewhat similar account of Tong, about this time, is found in "Modern Universal British Traveller."

"In the neighbourhood of Shifnall is a considerable village called Tong, where there is a most magnificent Castle....It at present belongs to the Duke of Kingston, and is a noble

---

[73] Sir Edward Stanley, "an arrant and dangerous Papist" died in 1632, but was not buried at Tong. According to his monument he married the Lady Lucy Percie, second daughter to Thomas Earl of Northumberland, and had one son and seven daughters. She and four daughters Arabella (18), Marie (16), Alis (15) and Priscilla (13) are buried under a monument in the church of Waltham, Essex. Thomas, the son, died in his infancy and is buried at Winwick, Lancashire. Petronella, Frances and Venesia were yet living in 1632. Frances married Sir John Fortescue of Seldon, Berks, Venesia married in 1625 Sir Kenelm Digby, and died May 1, 1633 aged 32, being buried in Christ Church, London, and Petronella died unmarried..

[74] There is no monument now in the chancel without an epitaph, that to Elizabeth, only daughter of Gervas, Lord Pierrepont having a long one – (see 1697) Mr. G. Griffiths suggests that the present monument is a composite one; the medallion commemorating Elizabeth Pierrepoint, the child's grandmother, who was buried at Tong 1656; the inscription commemorates Lucy Pierrepoint.

[75] The almshouses were founded by Lady Elizabeth Pembridge in 1411 and not by Lady Harris, who died in 1635.

structure. The front is particularly majestic; the towers are both lofty and handsome, while the fine battlements on the roof render the whole magnificently elegant... there are many ancient monuments in the church, particularly one to the memory of Sir Thomas Stanley, son of the Earl of Derby, and his lady, but although cut out of the most curious marble, yet it has been greatly defaced by the injury of time, and some of the figures have been broken off. At the west end of the church is a neat almshouse for six poor widows, who have an annual allowance of 40s., with a gown, shift and coals."

1764. In this year Tong changed owners; for Evelyn, 2nd Duke of Kingston, sold the property to Mr. George Durant. Mr. Durant was the son of the Rev. Josiah Durant, Rector of Hagley, Worcestershire, and had served with the expedition to Cuba in 1762. On purchasing the Tong estate he proceeded to spend great sums of money in its improvement including a complete system of irrigation. He also greatly altered the castle, cutting off the two wings and encasing the front and back of Sir Henry Vernon's old brick building with stone.[76]

On Nov. 14, 1764 a deed for the election of new trustees for the Tong Charities was drawn up between Sir Hugh Briggs and John Stubbs (the two trustees surviving from the election of Dec. 14, 1734) of the 1st part; and the Rev. Scrope Berdmore, D.D., curate of Tong, of the 2nd part. By it Henry Bridgeman, Esq., Plowden Slaney, Esq., the Rev. John Brooke, clerk, the Rev. Theophilus Buckeridge[77], clerk, and Nathaniel Barrett, gent., were

---

[76] The great part [of Tong castle] was pulled down in 1764 when the present castle was erected on the original site. The present castle is a stately and noble pile, quite a Baronial Mansion of Gothic and Moorish architecture, crowned with turrets, pinnacles and two stately and lofty domes producing a grand and striking effect. It is nearly wholly composed of stone, and has two commanding fronts, the one east, the other west, both being about 180 feet in length. The depth of the castle is nearly 70 feet. [Catalogue of Sale, Sept. 11, 1855.]

[77] Theophilus Buckeridge s. of Wild B. gent and Theophila d. of George Hand of Lichfield, b. July 22, bap. at Cathedral Aug. 1, 1724, educ. at Lichfield G. S.; P. C. of Edingale 1748-91; Rector of Gresham cum Barsingham, Norfolk 1760; Master of St. John's hospital 1769; P. C. of Tong 1770; Rector of Mautby, Norfolk 1770; 1784 Principal surrogate of Diocese of Lichfield 1784; resided at

elected in the place of Robert Aglionby Slaney, the Rev. Francis West[78], and James Devey, all deceased.

*1766. July 25. **Daniel Holmes**, who was unfortunately kill'd at ye castle, buried.*
Probably the result of an accident during the taking down and rebuilding of the Castle.

1769. Among the papers in the church chest is "The Examination of Beatrice Baker, widow (a vagabond being apprehended in Nantwich in the county of Chester begging and wandering and behaving herself there after a disorderly manner) taken upon oath before Roger Comberbach Esq., one of His Majesty's Justices of the Peace for the said county the fifth day of July, 1769." She deposed that "About twenty six years ago she was married at the ffleet in London to Richard Baker an Irishman who never gained a settlement in England to her knowledge and belief. Says her Maiden's Name was Beatrice Jones and that she was born in the parish of Tongue in the county of Salop and that her parents dyed when she was very young, and says she has been informed that she was maintained and taken care of by the parish of Tongue till she was seven years old, and apprehends her settlement to be in the said parish of Tongue." Mr. Comberbach ordered "the Constables of Nantwich to cause the said Beatrice Baker to be whipt in the said township of Nantwich pursuant to an Act of Parliament in that case made for punishing vagrants and other disorderly persons, and then to convey her to the parish of Woore in the said county of Salop that being the

St John's Hospital. Married Margaret d. of Josiah Durant, Rector of Hagley, husband of his father's sister. Wife died Feb. 4, 1793, buried at Edingale. He was bur. at Edingale Dec. 29, 1803 leaving issue
    Charles, Archdeacon of Coventry, Canon Residentiary of Lichfield.
    Richard, P. C. of Edingale 1791; Rector of Beighton, Norfolk, 1802; Vicar of Stone, Staffs. 1804; Chaplain of Stafford Jail 1825.
    Lewis, Capt. Shropshire Militia, 28 Feb. 1808.
      [Portrait in Harwood's edit. of Erdeswick's Antiquities of Staffordshire.]
[78] Francis West, Vicar of Albrighton 1726-47, died Jan. 13, 1747-8 aged 55.

place in the next Precinct through which she ought to be sent in the direct way to the said parish of Tongue."

On the back of the paper is written
Shropshire to wit – Convey the within mentioned vagabond to Mare in the county of Stafford.

           Dated the 6th Day of July, 1769.   Rob. Davison.
 County of Stafford – To the Constable of Maer in the said county – convey the Within vagrant to Cheswardine in the county of Salop.

           Dated 7th July, 1769.   R. Sneyd.

Shropshire to wit - To the Constable of Pilston in the said county – convey the Within vagrant to Pilston within the said county of Salop.

           Dated 10 July 1769.   P. Broughton.

Beatrice Baker was again examined on her arrival at Tong on July 17 1769 before Mr. Humphry Pitt, when she added to her above statement that she was fourty five years old and that her husband, a seafareing man, died at sea in March last.

1770. George Durant, Capt. Shropshire Militia 20 May, 1770.

1774. Quarter Sessions. April. Coroner's inquisition. Woman, lunatic, poisoned herself with white arsenic (Tong).

1775. Quarter Sessions. April. True Bill against George Durant, Esq., for digging a pool across highway at Tong.

1776. The old churchyard cross (see 1635) was apparently turned into a sundial this year, for it bears the inscription "Thos. Ore fecit 1776" – He was a clockmaker and several of his clocks are still to be found in the neighbourhood marked "Ore, Tong". He also played the clarionett in Tong Church.

1778. *June 20, buried George Durant Esq. (Abbey Church Register, Shrewsbury.)*

Oct. 24,1791. Benjamin s. of John and Mary Ward bap. This was :-
The Rev. Benjamin Ward, Missionary at Baddegama in Ceylon, 1818-28; Vicar of Ch. Ch., Carlisle 1831-59; Rector of Meesden, Herts, 1859-74; Hon. Canon of Carlisle Cathedral 1857; who died in 1874. He wrote in an unpublished autobiography "I was born on the 19th October, 1791, in the parish of Tong. My father was a farmer. He occupied the New Building farm for many years, and afterwards that adjoining it, the Park farm. I was the third of six sons. My education was the best that my parents could afford to give me. It was very poor, far inferior to what is now (1856), given in our national schools. I do not remember to have had any instruction in grammar or geography, much less in classics. I was taught to measure land and was fond of exercise. At the age of 16 I was apprenticed to a mercer and grocer at Welling-ton, and in January 1814 went up to London. My godmother was Mrs. Plowden of Hatton Hall and formerly of Tong Castle. (Edmund Plowden of Plowden had an only child Anna Maria. He succeeded to the Plowden estate in 1766, and died in 1838. During the minority of George Durant he lived at Tong Castle.)

1781. Randal Andrews of Tong, farmer, and overseer of the par-ish for 1781, was ordered by a vestry meeting to sell 115 oak trees and 47 ash trees then growing on ground belonging to the Poor of the Parish of Tong at **Herriott Hays** in the parish of Al-brighton, to Thomas Meeson, of Albrighton, timber merchant for the sum of £100.

1784. Nov. 5. Lucy daughter of Abraham and Lucy Hare buried.
Formerly there must have been a monument in the church to her. For, as stated in the European Magazine of January 1789 (quoted in Shropshire Notes and Queries vol. 1) her father, Abraham Hare of Bridgenorth, exciseman, "an untutored son of the Muses," according to the gentleman who sent it to the maga-zine, wrote this epitaph for it.

Here lies the body of Lucy Hare
Who departed this life 1784 aged 19 years.

In solemn silence, sweet repose,
Virtue and youth these stones inclose,

The sacred path of truth she trod,
Death snatched her hence to meet her God;
Eternal joys through Christ to share,
Prepared for all as Lucy Hare.

1789. A notice in the **Gentleman's Magazine** (Quoted in Bloxam's 'Companion to Gothic Architecture') speaking **of Tong Church** says

"The gallery with the entrance to the choir is yet unremoved, and the organ case remains, with little more room than was left for the player. This organ, to judge by what is left of it, seems the most ancient of the sort that has come under my observation, which for the entertainment of your musico-mechanical readers I will describe. And first the case. It is in the true gothic with pinnacles and finials after the manner of ancient tabernacles, and very like the one just finished and erected in Lichfield cathedral, only on a smaller scale. Now as to the other parts. The keys are gone but the sounding-board remains, and is pierced for one set of pipes only, seemingly an open diapason, whether of metal or wood could not be determined, there not being a single pipe left; from the apparent position and distance I presume they were of metal. I perceived no registers or slides for the other stops and observed the compass to be very short, only to A in alto for the treble part, and short octaves in the lower bass; therefore no more than 40 tones in the whole. The bellows were preserved in a lumber room near the vestry, double winded without folds, and made with thick hides, like unto a smith's or forge bellows. Thus simply constructed there could be no transmutation of sounding pipes, nor that variation to be produced from a mixture of different flute and reed pipes which are made use of in the modern organ. An instrumental machine whose improvement has been the work of more than one century; at first very plain and un-compounded, like the generality of mechanical inventions. And this remark will serve to establish in some measure the antiquity of the Tong organ."

Was "the gallery with the entrance to the choir" the old rood loft? In the chancel arch are still to be seen the holes in which were fixed the beams of the rood loft gallery, and the doorway giving access to the loft is in the pillar over the pulpit.

Down to the days of the Rev. G. S. Harding a **barrel organ** was used in Tong Church, Woolley the clerk generally setting the tunes, but on one occasion some person had set it to the tune "Moll in the wood , and I fell out, And what do you think it was about etc." to the utter consternation of many of the congrega-tion and the great amusement of others. It was replaced by one which came from Lichfield Cathedral and which stood in Chan-cel on North side at east of stalls. This in its turn gave way to one bought by the proceeds of a series of concerts held at Tong castle. It was consecrated on April 3rd 1877, the Rev. E. J. Wrottesley of Brewood being the preacher.

1792. On one of the gravestones in Tong Churchyard is the fol-lowing inscription: "In memory of **William Perry** of Bury St. Edmunds, in the County of Suffolk, who was most unfortu-nately killed by the accidental discharge of a fowling piece at Tong Castle, November 9th, 1792, in the 31st year of his age, Re-quiescat in pace". This burial is thus entered in the register: *"1792, Nov. 12. William Perry, who was unfortunately killed by the accidental discharge of a gun in Tong Castle."* In explanation of this is the following note, by Mr. H. F. J. Vaughan in the Shropshire Archaeological Transactions, vol. ii (1879), p. 261:-

Mr. Edmund Plowden was tenant of the Tong Estate during the minority of the second George Durant. He had a companion, who had been brought up with him, been to the same college with him, and lived with him at Tong Castle. One day Mr. Plowden was sitting in one of the reading rooms or studies which adjoin the Library, and the windows which look out to the south across a path to the flower gardens, and then over the Castle pool. His friend, who had been out shooting, came with loaded gun along the garden walk, and so must pass the windows of the study, when presently a scuffle was heard, then a loud report, and the servants rushing into the reading room to ascertain the cause found the body of the unfortunate man, streaming with blood, lying lifeless upon the floor, while near stood Mr. Plowden, who explained that he had attempted to get through the window with his loaded gun which had exploded with fatal effect; hence the dark stains which at least a few years ago were visible on the floor of one of the reading rooms.

Shropshire Quarter Sessions, January, 1793. Coroner's Inquisition.
Man taking a gun through a certain window accidentally shot himself, Tong: Deodand (gun), £5.00[79]

*1793. May 22. **Benjamin Charnock Payne, Esq.**, formerly a Major in the 99ᵗʰ Regt; who married the widow of Mr. Durant, owner of Tong Estate, to whom he was an Executor, buried.*
Major Payne was buried in the Durant vault in the centre of the Chancel, and when it was opened in 1891, his coffin was found bearing the inscription "Died 14 May, 1793 aged 38." Evans view of the castle published in 1789, is styled "Tong Castle in Shropshire, the seat of Benj. Charnock Payne, Esq." He left a daughter by his wife, stepdaughter of Mr. Durant.

---

[79] Any personal chattel which was the immediate cause of an accidental death was forfeited to the crown and called a Deodand. The Coroner's jury had to present what particular chattel was such cause, and to put a value on it. The right of the Crown to Deodands was given up in 1846.

Evans' view of the Castle published in 1789 is styled "Tong Castle in Shropshire, the seat of Benj. Charnock Payne. Esq." – see page 139.

1793. The following bill is among other overseer's papers and is interesting as shewing a doctor's fees a hundred years ago.

1793. Nanny Broughall, per order of Mr. Clarke, to Stanier and Bennett.

May 17	A bleeding	0	1	0
	An embrocation	0	1	0
	A Balsamic Mixture	0	1	6
	Flannell ¼	0	1	4
May 18	A Large Balsamic Mixture	0	2	4
	An Opening Draught	0	1	0
May 19	Do. Repd.	0	1	0
	A Dose of Opening Pills	0	0	6
May 20	A Mixture for a Glyster	0	1	0
	A Pipe and Bladder	0	0	6
May 21	The Balsamic Mixture repd.	0	2	4
May 24	A Journey to Tong	0	2	6
	A Plaister for the Ribs	0	1	0
May 27	A Journey	0	2	6
	The Balsamic Mixture repd.	0	2	4
June 3	A Journey	0	2	6
	A Pectoral Linctus	0	2	0
		1	6	4

1794 Jany. 17th. Settled the above. Sam. Bennett.
Apparently she was cured, for Ann Broughall, widow, was not buried till Jan.14, 1797.

1794. Sept. 25. John Huffadine, unfortunately drowned in a ditch near the Broom croft, buried.
Shropshire Quarter Sessions, Oct. 1794. Coroner's Inquisition. Man walking near brook fell in, Tong.

1796. April 1. Mary Lee, a servant at Tong Castle, who drowned herself in the S. Pool there; lunacy, buried.

May 20. Henry Hallam, juvenis, unfortunately killed by a horse at Uffoxey, buried.

Foul play having been suspected with regard to Mary Lee's death, tradition says that a **trial by ordeal** was made and many people were ordered to approach the corpse with the idea that if the murderer came near a change in it would take place.
Shropshire Quarter Sessions, April, 1796. Coroner's Inquisition. Woman, lunatic, drowned herself, Tong.[80]

1799. Feb. At Tong Castle, Charles Durant, Esq., to Miss Eld, daughter of Francis Eld, Esq., of Slighford. [Monthly Magazine, vol. 7, p. 169, March, 1799] There are two mistakes in this notice, Charles should be George, and Slighford should be Seighford. It is not entered in the Tong Register.

1799. Oct. 5. Francis Humpage, unfortunately suffocated by intoxication, buried.
Shropshire Quarter Sessions, Oct. 1799. Coroner's Inquisition. Man was drinking strong beer and drank a large quantity, by reason whereof he became quite disguised in liquor and was then and there suffocated. Tong.

1800. The Gentleman's Magazine of 1800, part ii p. 934, contains a notice, signed G., of Tong Church, in which it is said "The same stairs that lead up to the pulpit[81], lead also into the steeple,

---

[80] Early in the present century one of the maids at Tong Castle was found drowned in the ornamental water in the grounds under circumstances that led to the suspicion of foul play. Her master, the then eccentric Squire of Tong, whose fantastic buildings remain to bear witness to his peculiarities, made all his family, household and retainers come one by one to look at and touch the body, that the blood oozing from its nostrils might cause the murderer to be detected. But the keeper did not come. "The Squire was very fond on 'im and sent him awee of an arrant for 'im that dee, o' puppus, to get 'im out of the wee, loike! And so the ordeal failed!" (Miss Burne, Shropshire Folklore, p. 297. edit of 1883) Richard Jenks (sometimes spelled Ginx) was the supposed murderer, and confessed to F. O. Durant on his deathbed.
[81] A beautiful series of water colour drawings of Tong Church, by David Cox, jun, are in the possession of the Earl of Bradford. One of them shews a three decker pulpit with a sounding board (removed after 1855 during the incumbency of the Rev. G. S. Harding.) The pews are also shewn, much out of repair. The date of the drawings would be about 1845. David Cox jun., was born 1819, was a water colour artist of some repute, and died in 1885.

in which are a ring of six bells, the ropes of which hang down to the nave...In the church the pews are much out of repair, and should be renewed; but there are several curious monuments and memorials of the dead, among which I noticed one of alabaster to the memory of a Vernon. The effigies lie on an altar tomb, and had the remains of a **garland of flowers** (then nearly reduced to dust) round the neck and breast. The sexton told me that on every Midsummer day a new garland was put on, and so remained until the following, when it was annually renewed." Cf Cole.

This is an interesting example of an enduring custom. Roger la Zouche, Lord of Tong, who died in 1238 granted unto Henry de Hugefort and his heirs, three yardlands, three messuages and certain woods in Norton and Shaw in the parish of Tong with other privileges, in return for the rendering to the said Roger and his heirs of a Chaplet of Roses upon the Feast of the Nativity of St. John the Baptist (June 24) in case he or they shall be at Tong, if not it was to be put upon the image of the Blessed Virgin in the Church of Tong. This quitrent is mentioned also in 1284. No doubt on the image being removed at the reformation the wreath was put on a tomb near (see Mr. Cole's note in 1757). As the Marrion family were the only freeholders in Tong Norton in 1800, it is possible they were the heirs of de Hugefort and kept up the old custom, which is now abolished[82], the Earl of Bradford being the sole landowner in Tong Norton having purchased the Marrion property some 20 years ago. Dame Pembruge also in 1446 granted "a burgage with a croft at the end of the town of Tonge towards Culsals" to Thomas Scot for life, for the quitrent of a red rose on the feast of St. John the Baptist.

1801 Man much disguised in liquor fell from horse and dislocated his neck. Tong. (Quarter Sessions)

1802. On Sept. 4th 1802 an Indenture for the appointment of

---

[82] [This is a surprising comment from John Auden. Commenting now in 2004 we note that the custom has long been practised in 'recent' years].

new Charity Trustees was drawn up between the Rev. Theophilus Buckeridge of the city of Lichfield, clerk (the sole survivor of the trustees appointed in 1764) of the first part; William Chester Glover, of Lizard Grange in the parish of Tong, gentleman, and James Jones of Tong Norton, in the same parish, schoolmaster, (churchwardens of Tong) and Cornelius Higgins of Tong Norton, farmer, and Francis Downing of the same place, Innkeeper, (Overseers of the Poor), of the second part; and the Right Hon. Orlando, Lord Bradford, of Weston under Lizard in the co. of Stafford, Robert Slaney of Hatton Grange in the co. of Salop, Esq., George Brooke, of Haughton in the said co. Esq., Francis Eld, of Seighford in the co. of Stafford, Esq., and John Bishton, the younger, of Kilsall, in the co. of Salop, Esq., of the third part. By it the five last were chosen and appointed as trustees in the place of Henry Bridgeman, Lord Bradford, Plowden Slaney, the Rev. John Brooke, and Nathaniel Barrett all deceased.[83]

Because there was only one of the old trustees living, the Churchwardens and Overseers were associated with him in the election of five new trustees. This speaks of the Almshouses, and the school and the schoolmaster's house as being still at the west end of the Church, where they were in 1764, but it must have been soon after then that Mr. Durant removed them to other places on his estate. For the Charity report of 1820 says that soon after Mr. Durant came into the property, which he did in 1764, he removed the school and almshouses.

In 1806 considerable work was done at Tong Church for Jeffrey Heayse, a wheel-wright of Tong Norton entered in his accounts

1806	G. Durrant Esq., paint and numbering the seats in the church and chancel	0 18 6	
	Altering the cottage numbers, and in the church	0 2 6	
	Numbering the cottages at Tong	0 1 6	

[83] Sir Henry Bridgeman who succeeded his father as 5th baronet in July 1764, was created Baron Bradford in August 1794, and died June 5, 1800. Plowden Slaney died 1788.

Marking coffers in the church	0	2	6
Printing a large board in the vestry	1	11	6

1809. January Quarter Sessions. *Coroner's Inquisition. Man found dead from inclemency of weather, Tong.*
1809. April Woman or girl sitting by fire and her clothes took fire, *Tong.*

1809. In the grounds of Tong Castle, now fast falling to pieces, is a cenotaph bearing this inscription:- to the memory of Lieut. Jno. Henry Beaufoy of the 7th Regt. of Foot or Royal Fusiliers, who was killed while bravely defending a pass in a wood at the battle of Talavera.
"Lieut. Jno. Henry Beaufoy, born 23rd of August 1789, died July 28, 1809."
Another cenotaph stood once in the Castle Wood. "M. S. H. Hamilton Acre. Imp. Afric. Ob.: 1808: Aet:- Fr: of: S. 1813." There were also some other lines which had subsequently been erased.

1809. The coach road through Tong was much altered this year, as may be seen from a map by William Yates dated 1809, now in the possession of Mr. D. Jones of Kilsall. It formerly ran close to the churchyard and the now ruined almshouses, where traces of it can still be seen to the north of the present road; the old road also ran close to Lizard Mill and at the back of Lizard Grange, close in front of the Lizard cottages.

1809. There are several notices concerning the balloting for the militia which for convenience sake may be spoken of here. The first is dated January 9, 1809, and is an order from the General Quarter Sessions held at Shrewsbury to the parish of Tong to pay to the Treasurer of the county of Lancashire the sum of £5. 1s. 4d., the allowance made to the family of Zachariah Woodward, a private Militia man, serving for the Parish of Tong. The receipt is dated July 10, 1810.

The second is dated Jan 9, 1810, and is an order from the Shrewsbury Quarter Sessions to pay to the county of Staffordshire £23.11s.0d. the allowance to the family of Benjamin Hostwich, a private Militia man serving for Tong. The receipt of this sum is dated July 10, 1810 and is signed Joshua Peele, County Treasurer.

The third is the examination at Plymouth on Feb 18, 1811 of William Ore, a Balloted man serving in the Militia of the county of Salop before Lord Bradford, colonel and deputy Lieutenant, and R. Betton, Major and Deputy Lieutenant. He declares that he has not received the Bounty allowed by Government to Militia men, not having been enrolled in time to be entitled thereto. Therefore the parish of Tong is ordered to pay to William Ore, of the said Parish, servant, the sum of £12. 12s. 0d.

The fourth is a notice dated March 6, 1811, to say that at the last ballot, John Swann, and William Morris were balloted for Shifnal, Tong and Albrighton classed together. Swann paid the fine of £20 and was thereby excused, and William Morris was too short. Therefore no man was enrolled and the fine for which Tong was liable was £1 13s. 4d. At the same ballot Charles Thornton and John Salter were drawn for Tong, Donington and Albrighton classed together. Thornton paid the £20 and Salter was infirm and unfit for service, so that there was again a deficiency. The share of the fine of £40 upon Tong is £5 and the two sums make a total of £6.13s. 4d.

The last is a notice that the Bounty for Local Militia men for Tong at 2 guineas per man amounts to £30. 6s. 7d. And it is suggested that the amount be remitted to the county Treasurer to be paid by him on the order of the commanding officer on the inrolment of the men, so that the inconvenience of a Ballot, and the Fine on those balloted and not inrolled, as also the Fine of £15 per man upon the Parish for every man not inrolled may be avoided. It is dated Shrewsbury, April 8, 1813.

1810. The only other Churchwarden's Book besides that of 1630-80, begins

"The Accounts of Edward Phillips, Churchwarden from the Spring Visitation 1810 to the Spring Visitation 1811."
1810

June 6	For a new surplice	3	12	6
July 20	For cleaning the organ	2	12	6
Nov. 5	The ringers		12	0
Dec. 8	Mr. Underhill's bill for the Tenor Bell	137	11	0
Dec. 25	Psalmsingers	1	1	0

Sold the old Bell for £66. 14.0.

The present Tenor bell bears the inscription "Thomas Mears of London, 1810."

1811

June 8	Sacramental wine and two bottles	9	2
Oct. 20	Sacramental wine	9	0

Heaze's accounts contain
1811

Assisting with the commandments in the church
and materials   4   6

The commandments and the Lord's Prayer painted on reed canvas and framed in wood were on the east walls till the restoration of 1892. Possibly the stone canopies on either side of the east window were destroyed for their erection.

1812

Jan. 24	Sacramental wine	9	0
March 29	Sacramental wine	9	0
April 26	Expenses to Lightmoor to enquire for quarries for the churchfloor	5	0

Heaze enters

1812   Framing, boarding, and making, and
materials; a coal and coak cupboard in
the vestry   3   19   0
Making a ladder to go up to the Li-
brary   9   6

This cupboard was in use till the Restoration in 1892. In March
1812, according to the Charity Commissioners Report of 1820 the
Library was examined and the number of books then in it compared with the number in the catalogue.

William Woolley paid school salary March to Easter.

**According to the Official Report of Tong Parish of the Expense
and Maintenance of the Poor etc. made to the Government in
1815**

Item	Easter 1813	Easter 1814	Easter 1815
Money raised by Poor or other Rates	414	431	499
Expended			
Law, Removals, Journeys, Overseers	10	12	12
Poor Maintenance	171	167	194
Militia, families of militia men	19	1	24
Other Expenses		4	
Church, Highway, County	213	246	269
Total Expended	*414*	*431*	*499*

Property Tax – value of Property	4050	4050	4050

Permanent Relief to Persons out of work	17	18	16
Persons in Workhouse	7	6	6
Persons receiving Occasional Relief	5	8	7
Friendly Society members	17	19	20

Average Charity under Parish Officers	£23	4s.	0d
Other Purposes	£55	16s	0d

Almshouse for 6 Poor Widows and a School

1812. May 12. Mr. Reynolds for carpet, bosses etc. for the chancel £25. 0s .6d.

Memorandum. The undersigned Parishioners of Tong attended this day, April 19, 1812, according to a Public Notice sent round the Parish, to inspect the repairs going on at the church, and do Unanimously approve of the same and recommend that the carriage of the materials shall be done by the Parishioners; that the cieling of the church shall be whitewashed all over, and that the church door shall be cut down the middle, and to give James Piatt fifteen pounds according to his Proposal for the workmanship (No signatures.)

1813. At a meeting held in the vestry this 17th day of January, 1813 the following **rules and regulations for Tong School** were approved by us.[signed] W. H. Molineux, Minst., James Jones, John Titley, Churchwardens, William Ward, Francis Weaver, Overseer, W. Bishton, Edward Phillips, John Ward, Joseph Peel, G. Durant, Benjamin Yardley.

All the scholars to be taught Reading, Writing and accounts, and the girls knitting and sewing. School hours in winter in the morning from eight to twelve, and in the evening from two to four. In the summer in the morning from seven till nine and ten till twelve. In the evening from two till five. Holydays, one week at Easter, four weeks at Harvest, and two weeks at Christmas.

Any child living in the parish, or belonging to it to be received into the school with a Ticket from the minister and churchwardens; their respective ages to be laid on the vestry table once in a quarter on the Sunday after the quarter day.

All the scholars to be brought by the master to church every Sunday.

At a meeting held this 19th day of April, 1813, being Easter Monday, in consequence of the resolution of the parish meeting held the 17th day of January last, the election of a successor to the late Robert Tagg[84] in the free school was deferred till this day; when Andrew Cousins, officiating clerk of the parish was elected to the Sunday and free School being unanimously approved of from his having a most irreproachable character for honesty, sobriety, morality and piety. His unremitting attention in the discharge of his duty as clerk, his mildness of manners, steadiness of conduct, industrious habits, and neatness of Person, rendering him an unexceptionable candidate for the situation. It is resolved that the rules and regulations for the free school made the 17th of January last, be strictly adhered to. (signed) W. H. Molineux, Minister, James Jones, Churchwarden, Edw. Phillips, Constable, Fra. Weaver, Geo. Vaughan, Overseers, J. Ward, Walter Marrion, G. Durant.

April 29	Mr. Dovey for giving assistance to procure the new Bell in Tune, by a vestry order	1	1	0
May 26	Paid Mr. Smith, for Quarries	32	10	4
Sept. 2	Mr. Marrian for maintenance of Lockley's men while repairing the church	9	12	2
Dec. 24.	Mr. Lockley, Plumber, in part	15	0	0
Dec. 27.	For 12 dozen sparrow heads		4	0

---

[84] Robert Tagg, Tong, aged 77, buried Jan. 16, 1813.

1813. Heaze enters

New Bottoming the Bier and repd. it	5	9
Painting and lengthening the double doors in the porch	1 7	6
Do. the wicket with green	11	6

1814 In Oct. **1814,** acting as trustees of the Tong Charities, the Rev. William Hamilton Molineux, of Ryton in the co. of Salop, clerk; James Jones of Tong Norton, in the said co., malster, and Francis Weaver of the parish of Tong, miller, for £180, purchased from John Weaver, of Northfield, in the co. of Worcester, yeoman, a tenement at Horsebrooke in the manor of Brewood.

1814. Received this 4th day of January, 1814 of George Jellicoe, Esquire, of Little Chatwell for the admittance of his uncle, the late George Jellicoe, Esquire[85], to be buried in the church at Tong £10.0.0

Oct. 2	Mr. Benjamin Thomas for four new wheels to the bells etc.	10	10	0
Oct. 27	Mr. Lockley in full	57	19	9¾

Nov. 6. The accounts seen and allowed by us first deducting the ten pounds received of Mr. Jellicoe, which is given by the Rev. Mr. Muckleston to pay for the King's Arms in stone to be put up in the church[86]. It was also ordered that the ch.warden do apply to the Artificial Stone Manufactory, Lambeth, for the King's Arms to be erected in a conspicuous place in the church. (signed) W. H. Molineux, Min., G. Durant, Franc Weaver, Walter Marrian, James Jones.

---

[85] George Jellicoe of Chatwell, senex, buried July 10, 1812.
[86] In memory of the retirement of Napoleon to Elba, and the Peace of Paris, May 30, 1814.

The Kings Arms made of artificial stone invented by Eleanor Coade (1733-1821).
Other examples of Coade stone may be found at St George's Windsor and Bucking-
ham Palace.

1815.

June 14	Mr. William Davies of Shiffnall for repairing the church clock and putting a dial thereto	29	2	0
Sept. 29	Letter demanding the money for the Iron Chest			4
Oct. 12	Carriage of the King's Arms from London	3	12	4
Nov. 10	Mr. Wilson, Expenses from and to London, he having put up the King's Arms	5	0	0

In 1815 the present Offoxey or New Road was made by Mr. Durant.

According to the M.S. of the late Rev. R. G. Lawrence, Vicar of Tong 1870-76,

> "at the time the road was made from Tong Norton to Tong Rough, land called the Poor's Land was sold by order of, and purchased by, Mr. Durant, and added to the Knowle

Farm. The land is known now as the Marsh Fields and lies opposite to the old Parish Workhouse. The money received was spent in making the new road. Land also belonging to the poor of Tong near the White Oak, and now part of the Meeshill Farm, was treated in the same way for the same purpose. After these wholesale proceedings the board containing the account of the charitable gifts to the parish, which stood in the vestry, was removed by one Huffadine, a village carpenter".

The following is a copy of the Order closing the old roads.
"Shropshire April Sessions, 1815. At this Sessions was filed an Order of two Magistrates with the consent of the landowner for diverting a Haighway through lands belonging to George Durant, Esq. of Tong Castle in this county:-

We, Robert Slaney Esq., and Thomas Lloyd, Clerk, two of His Majesty's Justices of the Peace for the said county, at a Special Sessions held at Tong in the Hundred of Brimstree in the said county, on the 23rd. Day of February, 1815, having upon view, found that a certain part of the Highway within the parish of Tong in the said Hundred lying between the north-west corner of the Holt Wood, and the Norton and Weston road, at the Knowle Sand-pit, being of the length of 3175 yards, and from the aforesaid north-west corner of the Holt Wood by the Holt, Hubbal, and Hill Farms to the Village of Tong, being of the length of 3906 yards, or thereabouts, may be diverted and turned, so as to make the same nearer and more commodious to the Public; and having viewed a course proposed for the new Highway in lieu thereof, through the lands and grounds of George Durant Esq. of Tong Castle, of the length of 2878 yards, and of the breadth of 24 feet or thereabouts; and having received evidence of the consent of the said George Durant Esq. to the said new Highway being made through his lands hereinbefore described, by writing under his hand and seal: We do hereby order that the said

Highway be diverted and turned through the lands aforesaid; and we do order an equal assessment not exceeding the
rate of sixpence in the pound, to be made, levied and collected upon all and every the occupiers of lands, tenements,
woods, tithes, and hereditaments in the said Parish of Tong,
and that the money arising therefrom be paid and applied to
the making of the said new road.

Given under our hands and seals at Tong this 23rd. Day of
February, 1815.

Thomas Lloyd   Robt. Slaney.

*I, George Durant, of Tong Castle, in the County of Salop, Esq., being
owner of the lands through which part of a certain Highway, lying between the Holt Wood and the Workhouse at Tong Norton in the Parish
of Tong is intended to be directed and turned, in consideration of receiving the land of the old Highway in lieu thereof, do hereby consent
to the making and continuing of such new Highway through my said
lands;*

Given under my hand and seal this 23rd. Day of February, 1815

G. Durant.

We, whose names are subscribed, being the Justices of the Peace,
who viewed the several Highways described, and made an Order for diverting the old Highway, and being satisfied that the
new Highway is properly made and fit for the reception of travellers, do hereby order the said old Highway from the north
west corner of the Holt Wood to the crossing of the road from
Tong Norton to Weston, being of the length of 3175 yards and
the breadth of 18 feet upon a medium, also the road from the
south end of the Holt Lane to the crossing of the White Lady
road, near the south angle of the said Holt Wood being of the
length of 320 yards and breadth of 18 feet at a medium, and also
the road from the aforesaid north west corner of the Holt Wood,
to the village of Tong by the Holt, Hubbal and Hill Farms, being
of the length of 3906 yards and breadth of 18 feet at a medium to
be stopped up, and the land and soil thereof to be given to

George Durant Esq. of Tong Castle, in lieu of the land given up by him for the New Road.

Reserving , nevertheless, to Edward Phillips, and his heirs, proprietors of his freehold in Tong, a free passage for persons, horses, cattle and carriages through the lands and soil of the said old Highway to and from the said Free-hold land of the said Edward Phillips to the village of Tong, according to his ancient usage thereof[87].

Given under our hands and seals at Tong this 16th day of March 1815.
Thomas Lloyd. Robt. Slaney.

The map which accompanies the order is inscribed "Termination of a New Road in the Parish of Tong and county of Salop from Bishops Wood in the county of Stafford to the village of Tong Norton being 2 miles 3 furlongs 4 yards, through the estate of G. Durant Esq. commenced October 1809. Completed February 1815.
George Hempenstall, surveyor."

		£	s	d
1816 April 1.	Paid for a letter from London demanding the money for the King's Arms[88]		1	1
	Do. demanding the money for the Iron Chest			5
1817 June 7.	Pd. Mr. Fisher Mr. Cole's Bill for the King's Arms	65	3	0

1819 At a Vestry held this 14th day of March. It was resolved that a rate of 2d in the pound be collected to defray the expenses up to Easter 1819, and that the churchwardens do employ Mr. Mott to collect the arrears specified. [signed] W. H. Molineux, J. Stanier.

---

[87] The name of Edward Phillips is found in the church rate book till 1820; and Mr. Thomas Wood of Wolverhampton paid on "the tythes of Mr. Phillips' land" from 1820 to Aug, 1832 inclusive. No doubt Mr. Phillips sold his land this year to Mr. Durant. One of the pews in Tong Church near the font has painted on it a large E.P.
[88] [The Royal Arms, made of Coade ware, set on the north wall]

In 1819 a Brief throughout the country was issued for loss by fire at Meeshall, Tong, the damage done being estimated at £700.

1820 Jan 7   Mr Harris' Bill for the Iron Chest £6.11.6; postage of letter 4d.   6   11   10

About the year **1820**, there lived at **Lizard Grange a very wicked farmer**. And when he died there was a great storm of wind, and noises heard all over the house, and doors banging without any cause, so that no-one could stay in the house except one man, who was bribed with as much spirit as he liked to drink, to sit up in one of the lower rooms with a good fire. And the horses in the stable were all so restless and excited that they had to be let out to go where they would, lest they should kick the stalls down. All this went on till after the corpse had been removed. And, after that, many said the farmer came again, for they had met him riding on his black pony. (Shropshire Folklore p.123.)

1821 In the Overseer's Rate book, April 23, 1820 to July 1836, is the following list of **houses paying rates in 1821**:- Tong Castle, The Hill Farm, The Grange Mill, Vicarage, Offoxey, Tong Lodge, New Bell Tong Norton, Ruckley, Uffadine Tong Norton, Meace Hill, Holt farm, Hubbal, Bush Tong Norton, (Francis Downing Overseer from May 1821), White Oak, (Mr. Vaughan, Overseer from May 1821), Tong Knoll, Ruckley Wood, The Grange House, Old Bell Tong, Lowe Tong Norton, Tong Lodge West, Smith Tong Norton, Tong Park, New Building.

In the Church Rate Book, Easter 1821-23, is the following list:- Knoll, George Anslow; Ruckley, George Bishton; Lodge, Thomas Bishton; Ruckley Wood, Robert Cherrington; Forge, William Cherrington; Grange Meadow, Robert Dickin; Parsonage, John Glover; Hubbal, George Hempenstall; Offoxey, Richard Jones; New Building, Joseph Moore; Tong, Thomas Moore; Bell, William Moore; Tong Hill, John Norton; Meeshill, John Pastance; Grange Land, James Richards; Grange, John Stanier, Esq.; Holt Farm, Sam. Smith; White Oak Lodge, John Starkey;

White Oak, George Vaughan; Grange Mill, Francis Weaver.

1821. The present wall at the Convent Lodge drive to Tong Castle was built this year, for it bears the inscription "Posteritati sacrum impensis Geo. Durant an. 1821"[89]. The old coach road ran then close to the wall and across the old bridge, and the pulpit-like structure on the wall was intended for Mr. Durant to sit in, and speak with any friends who might be driving by. The Convent Lodge was so named because the woman who lived there, by order of Mr. Durant wore a nun's dress and sandals. The gates are said to have been originally made at Coalbrookdale for St. George's Hall, Liverpool. John Vaughan, a village workman, executed all the carving.

An order of the Shropshire Quarter Sessions, dated July 13, **1829,** speaks of "different **Prize fights** having taken place in this and the neighbouring Counties," and many serious offences having been committed, destructive of the Public Peace, injurious to the property and even endangering the lives of individuals, especially in the Parishes of Tong and Albrighton, as shown upon a late occasion."

For fetching the doctor to the Hurmet	1	0	Sept. 1821
Paid for a notis from Shiffnal to deliver in the Population	0	4	June 1821
Coroner's Inquests at the Bell for Eating and Ale	18	8	Nov22,1823
Expenses for striping and cleaning Sarah Picken	1	6	Aug.16,1823
Relieved a pasport sailor		6	Aug.20.
For new cloathing Sarah Picken and paid for making them	1 3	0	Aug. 22.

---

[89] [*Sacred to posterity, donated (erected at the expense of) by George Durant 1821*].

Population of the Parish of Tong taken by James Jones May 28, 1821

Inhabited Houses		100
Families	100	
Now building		0
Uninhabited Houses		2
Employed in agriculture	68	
Handicrafts	27	
Other families	5	
Males	261	
Females	275	
Total of Persons	536	
Verified upon Oath	3rd July 1821 James Jones	

1823 This year the churchwarden enters ;- Psalmsingers £2 12 0d
John Navils or Neville, Tong, aged 38 was buried on October 7 1823. Coroner's Inquest. Verdict, accidental death. (Register) He was house carpenter at Tong Castle and fell out of a tree in the stable yard while sawing off a branch.

This year **the Maltese Cross** marking the place where unbaptised children are buried was erected on the north side of the church. On the south side it bears the inscription G. D. – H. M. E. 1823. On the top the words – Chrysoms Cemetery. On the North side but fast becoming illegible:

But save the cross above my head
Be neither name nor emblem spread
By prying stranger to be read
Or stay the passing pilgrim's tread.

The Giaour: Byron

Weep not for those whom the veil of the tomb
In life's happy morning hath hid from our eyes,
Ere sin through a blight on the spirit's young bloom
Or earth hath profaned what was born for the skies.

Death chill'd the fair fountain ere sorrow had stain'd it,
Twas frozen in all the pure light of its course,
And but sleeps till the sunshine of heaven had unchained it
To water that Eden where first was its source.

T. Moore

Like the last beam of evening thrown
On a white cloud – just seen and gone.

1824

August 16 Joseph Doran, Tong, aged 52 buried. Coroner's Inquest, verdict, died by the Visitation of God.

Oct 27 James Hammersley, Emersley, or Hemmingsley, Lizard Forge, aged 43 buried. Coroner's Inquest, died by the Visitation of God.
Hemmingsley was a noted owner of fighting cocks, of whose prowess traditions still exist in Tong.

Oct 30 Hannah Reynolds, Almshouses, aged 37, buried. Coroner's Inquest, verdict, Accidental Death. Killed Oct 27 by the fall of one of the elm trees in the churchyard while gathering sticks during a violent storm.

The churchwarden's accounts contain the following entries

1826	Book of Offices		5	6
1829	Relieved 5 sailors in distress		5	0
1830	Pd. for ale to put down the hurdles to fence the churchyard		2	6
	George Durant Esq. in part towards fencing the churchyard gave	5	0	0
1831	Hurdles for the churchyard	15	4	0
	Psalmsingers	2	12	0
	Ale for the ringers		12	0

In regard to this **fencing of the churchyard**, the Rev. R. G. Lawrence in his M.S. says "The fence round the churchyard in which stood the present grand old elm trees[90], a ditch being on the Park side of it, was removed by order of Mr. Durant and an iron fence placed round the churchyard within the line of the trees so that they might be for the future in the Park." Probably it was at this time that the carriage drive to the castle was moved from close to the east side of the churchyard to its present position (see description of Vicarage grounds 1725) and the piece of land in front of the Vicarage given in exchange for the old Vicarage orchard.

1831 At the Census of 1831 the following return was made of Tong.

Inhabited Houses		99
Families	99	
Uninhabited Houses		2
Families employed in agriculture	61	
Families employed in trade	36	
All other families	2	
Total of families	99	
Males	253	
Females	257	
Males upwards of 20 years	145	
Agricultural occupier[91] 1st class	29	
Agricultural occupier 2nd class	11	
Labourers in agriculture	9	
Retail trades and handicrafts	36	
Labourers not agricultural	29	
All other males of 20 years	4	

[90] Three of these trees, including the two finest which stood on each side of the wicket leading from the castle to the church, were blown down by the gale of March 24, 1895, and the tops of four others were cut off, and now only one is left in its full height.

[91] Agricultural Occupiers of the 1st class were those who constantly employ and pay one or more labourers or farm servants in husbandry. While those in class 2 were occupiers of land who employed no labourers other than their own families.

Male servants upwards of 20 years	18
Male servants under 20 years	17
All female servants	29

There were 5 Blacksmiths, 4 Bricklayers, 3 Butchers, 2 Cabinet Makers, 7 Wheelwrights, 1 Clockmaker, 2 Hawkers, 1 Malster, 1 Miller, 4 Publicans, 4 Shoemakers, and 2 Tailors. Total Tradesmen 36.

The population of Tong in 1801 was 404; in 1821, 536; in 1831, 510; in 1851, 511; in 1871, 580; in 1881, 498; in 1891, 445; in 1901, 436.

1832. In the garden at Tong Priory is a cenotaph on which is carved:- M. S. Georgii Hamilton, Legione Regis Armigeri. In Bello et Pace Viginti Annos Gloriam Britanniae Consecravit. Nat: XIV Nov. MDCCLXX. Ob. 1832[92].

1834. *Oct. 28. George, son of Richard and Sarah Salter, Tong Castle, labourer, baptized.* Salter's cottage (at Tong Shaw) was burnt down in the summer and his wife was kindly accommodated with a room at the Castle during her confinement. (Bapt. register)[93]

1836. *On Tuesday the 5th of July the thermometer stood at 88 in the shade. R. Robinson. At 89 at ½ past 2. J. Dale.* (Bapt. Register)

1837. There existed for many years at Tong the **"Loyal Orange Club",** but to commemorate the accession of Queen Victoria, its

---

[92] [To the sacred memory of (M. S. is probably memoriae sanctae) George Hamilton, Knight in the forces of the King. In war and in peace he consecrated twenty years of his life for the glory of Britain. Born 14th November 1770. Died 1832.]

[93] The houses burnt were not at Tong Knowle, but at Tong Norton, (Childs' and Tipton). They were set fire to by S. Salter "whilst baking", the neighbours were J. and E. Chesney. The new houses were built, with church-like windows, a tablet in centre bearing "The Phoenix, 1834, G.D." This was taken out, and windows made as at present by the Earl of Bradford about 1870-1 on account of its resembling an ecclesiastical building.

name was changed to the Loyal Victoria Friendly Society. The feast was kept on June 20th or the Saturday following. This society was dissolved in 1885, its place being taken by the Court Tong Castle, no. 3903, Ancient Order of Foresters. The Foresters S. was founded about 1863.

1838. March 6th 1838. At a Vestry held in the Parish Church of Tong, R. Robinson in the chair: it was resolved (1) That on account of a meeting held on the 2nd day of May 1837 which authorised the repairs of the Church, the Churchwardens have carried the same into effect to the satisfaction of the Parish. Proposed by Mr. Durant and seconded by Mr. Hempenstall. (2) That in order to defray the expenses which have taken place, a rate be levied for Nine pence in the pound throughout the Parish. Proposed by Mr. Durant seconded by Mr. Picken.

R. Robinson, chairman. G. Durant. Thos. Picken. M. Bothams. Thos. Icke, and Wm. Earp, churchwardens. George Hempenstall. Richard Chesney.

The existing board in the vestry concerning the Tong Charities, was erected this year, in place of the one put up in 1806, and taken down about 1815. The vagaries of lettering and punctuation have not, however, been followed in this copy. The initials C.H. are those of Charles Huffadine, a wheelwright of Tong Norton[94].

Lady Harris	For apprenticing poor children	£100
Lady Pier-point	£4 per annum to teach poor girls to read – for their books £1, the remaining interest for the poor of the parish at the discretion of the Minister and Churchwardens	£200
Rev.	For the poor of the parish at the dis-	

---

[94] This board is said by Charles Huffadine, son of the 'C. H.' on board to have been antedated, and Mr. St. George said to Thomas Cherrington of Tong Forge, concerning it and the business of the charities transacted at the meeting "the Squire has this day sown damnation to his own soul and mine also."

Mr. Peitier	cretion of the Minister and church-wardens	£100

The above benefactions were consolidated to purchase a small farm of 31 acres, 3 roods, 2 poles in the parish of Albrighton which yielded £14 in 1746 and raised £48 in 1835.

Annual Income

	From the above	£48
Duke of King-stone	From the Tong Castle Estate for the teaching of 10 poor boys and a house for the master with 24 poles of land.	£4
Duke of King-stone	For six poor widows, six houses and 1 rood, 3 poles of land.	
Lord Pierpont	From the Tong Castle Estate for the six widows	£12
Lord Pierpont	From the Tong Castle Estate to buy wool to be worked up by the poor and when woven to allow each widow a gown, the rest to be given to the other poor.	£12
Lord Pierpont	From the Tong Castle Estate to buy hemp, to be worked up by the poor and then sold to apprentice poor children.	£10
	A subscription of £142. 16s. was made in 1805 to increase the schoolmaster's salary.	
	A house and 1 acre, 3 roods, 2 poles of land was purchased with it at Horsebrooke in 1815 with the assistance of money received for timber from the poors land.	£10
	C.H. 1838.	

"It having been found by the Trustees that for the most part those apprenticed rarely stuck to the trade to which they were articled, the Trustees resolved in 1873 that the money should go to the schoolmaster's salary" (R. G. L)

The timber had been sold in 1781 for £100.

1839. This year Mr. Durant gave to Tong Church a silver paten bearing his crest, a fleur-de-lis, and the inscription "The gift of George Durant, Tong Castle, 1839"; and also a silver pocket communion service bearing the same words.

At a meeting of the inhabitants of the parish of Tong held at the vestry on Thursday the 21st of February 1839, pursuant to notice affixed on the church doors on Sunday the 17th instant by Richard Chesney, Clarke, of which the following is a copy :- "Tong, 17th February, 1839, a meeting of the inhabitants of this parish is requested at the vestry on Thursday morning next the 17th instant at 10 o'clock to lay a church rate.

Rev. Joseph Dale, Officiating Minister. Thomas Icke, William Earp, Churchwardens."

A church rate was laid at the rate of nine pence in the pound upon the last assessment. Proposed by G. Durant, Esq., seconded by Thos. Picken. G. Durant, Thomas Picken, John Holding, M. Bothams, G.Hempenstall, Thomas Icke, Churchwarden.

Objected to as an exorbitant and unnecessary rate, John Broughall.

August 29, 1839. Proceedings of a meeting held this day in consequence of a notice given by the churchwardens on Sunday last to report to the parishioners their inability (sic) to collect the last church rate in consequence of the refusal of the undermentioned inhabitants of the parish objecting to pay their share of it. [Here follow seven names but a page has been torn out.] It is therefore the unanimous opinion of this meeting that the churchwardens be empowered forthwith to recover the same according to law.

G. Durant, Leo. H. St. George, minister, M. Bothams, G. Hempenstall, John Harding, Wm. Earp and Thomas Icke, churchwardens.

1840. April 20. Easter Monday.

For cleaning walls and repairing the church.

Hally's bill	123	0	4½
Mr. Harly's bill for leading etc.	83	6	2
Law expenses	11	0	0
Total	217	6	6½
3 years expenses of church (ie Easter 1837 to Easter 1840)	44	15	2
Disbursed	262	1	8½
Amount of levy collected	125	12	4
Amount of subscription recd.	23	10	0
Amount of levy granted 20 April 1840	43	13	4
Total	192	15	8
Amt. Received	192	15	8
Amt. Due to Thos. Icke	69	6	0½

In April 1840, Charles Dickens began to publish his story of *The Old Curiosity Shop,* the closing scenes of which, as he himself told the late Archdeacon Lloyd [95], were laid at Tong. Dickens, while staying at Shrewsbury in November 1838 came over by coach (to Tong) and stayed at the Harp at Albrighton[96]. His description of Tong is, in the main, fairly accurate, though there is no armour preserved in the church, and no crypt or well to be found there, nor is there now a watermill in the village. Nor are the far away blue Welsh mountains to be seen. Probably Dickens meant the Wrekin, which is visible from the church porch. He is also hardly correct when he says in Chapter LV that "the castle in which the old family had lived was an empty ruin". Tong Castle, at the time Dickens visited the place, was not a ruin though it was empty. The married life of Mr Durant and his first wife was not a happy one, and resulted in a separation, after which he spent his time principally, on the continent near Paris,

---

[95] Percy Fitzgerald, Bozland, Dicken's Places and People, pp. 60-66
[96] S.A.S.T. Vol XI, Second Series p.150

where he had a villa. After her death in 1829 he married again, and his second wife preferred their continental home, or their town house in Kensington to the country, which had been the scene of so much that was painful. Consequently they resided little at Tong Castle, which, however, was kept ready for their reception whenever they might wish to visit it. [97].

"It was a fine, clear autumn morning when the schoolmaster and his two companions came to the village, and stopped to contemplate its beauties. 'See, here is the churchyard', cried the delighted schoolmaster, 'and that old building close beside is the schoolhouse' ... they admired everything. The old grey porch, the mullioned windows, the venerable gravestones dotting the green churchyard, the ancient tower, the very weathercock, the brown thatched roofs of cottage, barn and homestead peeping from among the trees. The stream that rippled by the distant water mill, the blue Welsh mountains far away. 'I must leave you somewhere for a few minutes,' said the schoolmaster, 'where shall I take you?' To the little inn yonder?' 'Let us wait here,' rejoined Nell. 'The gate is open. We will sit in the church porch until you come back.' 'A good place, too,' said the schoolmaster, leading the way towards it, disencumbering himself of his portmanteau and placing it on the stone seat. The child watched him from the porch until the intervening foliage hid him from her view, and then stepped softly out into the old churchyard. It was a very aged, ghostly place. The church had been built many hundreds of years ago, and once had a convent or monastery attached; four arches in ruins, remains of oriel windows, and fragments of blackened walls were yet standing".
(Chap. XLVI)

Some part of the edifice had been a baronial chapel, and here were effigies of warriors stretched upon their beds of stone with folded hands ... the child left the chapel very slowly and often turning back to gaze again; and coming to a low door which

---

[97] S.A.S.T. Vol. ii. (1879)

plainly led into the tower, she opened it, and climbed the winding stair in darkness, save where she looked down, through narrow loopholes, on the place she had left, or caught a glimmering vision of the dusty bells. At length she gained the end of the ascent and stood upon the turret top. Oh the glory of the sudden burst of light; the freshness of the fields and woods stretching away on every side; and meeting the bright blue sky; the cattle grazing in the pasture; the smoke that coming from among the trees seemed to rise upward from the green earth, the children at their gambols down below, ... It was like passing from death to life; it was drawing nearer Heaven." (chap LIII)

Dickens' grandmother was housekeeper at Tong.

Many postcards a century ago showed these cottages as they were then, describing them as 'Little Nell's Cottage.'

1842. John Martin for plastering a blank door   12s. 6d.

This was the west door of the church, and when it was re-opened in 1892, it was found that the plaster concealed very rough boarding which filled up the doorway, and in the boarding a small door, fitted with hinges, but only 4½ feet high. On the boards was written in chalk "George Hempenstall", the name of one of the churchwardens for 1841-2.

1844. During this year the parish of Tong was surveyed by Sir John Rennie, and Captain W. S. Moorsom, engineers of the Shrewsbury, Wolverhampton, Dudley and Birmingham Railway. It was proposed to run the line across the parish entering across the Lower Forge Pool (now an osier bed), past Tong Norton, where there was to be a station, then by Hubbal Grange, and out near White Ladies. This line was never made, an alternative route being eventually chosen in 1845, which only crossed a small portion of the parish at Ruckley Wood, the name too of the Railway company being altered into Shrewsbury, Wolverhampton and South Staffordshire Co. Another line was also surveyed through Tong, viz "the Shrewsbury and Leicester Direct Ry". It was to enter Tong at Timlett Hollow cross the Shrewsbury, Wolverhampton and Dudley Ry. at Tong Norton and then run on past the Knoll, taking somewhat the same line as the present park wall.

1845. In the March number of the Archaeological Journal for this year appeared an **illustrated article on Tong church by J. D. Pettit**. After describing the architectural details he ends his paper thus:

> "It is hardly to be supposed that so beautiful a church will long escape the process of restoration. Externally, some of the pinnacles are broken or displaced, and others have lost their finials. If these were renewed, after the model of such as are sufficiently perfect, to preserve this general effect, the latter being suffered to remain untouched, and other mutilations in the stonework, as in the tracery of the

west windows, carefully repaired, no doubt the general aspect would be improved. The same applies to the woodwork of the interior. Some of the poppy heads that have slightly suffered from decay might be preserved in their present state. Others might be restored and the barbarous work with which a few of them have been repaired, I suppose during the last or preceding century, might be replaced with work of a better character. The repair of the rood screen would require a careful and able artist, but in this it would be desirable to remove none of the present work that can possibly be kept in its place. In the nave several unsightly pews rise above the level of the original seats, and might be removed with great advantage to the appearance of the building. The original disposition of the seats does not seem to have been much disturbed except in one or two instances, and could easily be retained, as a very economical disposition of the space seems by no means required for the wants of the parish. The monuments admit of some repair, there being several fractures, especially in the most beautiful one, Sir Henry Vernon's. Some stoves too that are now in the body of the church by no means conduce to its beauty; and I would further suggest, that if the Golden Chapel must be used as a pew, some tapestry of the date or character of the 16th century, if any could be procured, of an appropriate description, might advantageously replace the present linings and curtains of cloth, and some good cinquecento painted glass be substituted for the modern coloured glass in its windows." (J. D. Pettit)

1848. While being rung on Ash Wednesday, 1848, the Great Bell was badly cracked and its tone spoiled.

Bagshaw's Gazeteer 1851. The Castle is now occupied by two female servants, the owner G. C. S. Durant Esq. being abroad. A feast is held at Tong on the Sunday before St. Matthew's day.

Mr. Durant's agent at the present time is holder of four of the largest farms in the parish viz Tong Park Farm, Hubbal Farm, Holt Farm and the Mees Farm.

Census. 1801, 404; **1831**, 510; **1841**, 536. The Earl of Bradford, Mrs. Celeste Durant, and Mr. William Jones, Bush Inn are also proprietors. The big bell remained entire till the first Wednesday in Lent 1849 when it cracked when tolling for divine service.

Tong Taverns

The Bell - 'Tong' E. Phillipps (initials on pew) Moore.

The Bell - Tong Norton Radenhurst, G. Bennion, R. Lees, H. Page (Each of these married Sarah Smith, she died at Seven Stars, Beckbury, her father being a blacksmith and publican, Tong Norton). Mrs. Jones (née Marrion) succeeded the Pages, then A. Leach, C. Stanley, M. Davies. G. Bennion, R. Lees, W. Jones, A. Leach, C. Stanley and M. Davies all died there.

'Horse Shoes'- Tong Norton, kept by Smith (now H. Balls.) *by the blacksmith's shop.*

Bush - Marrion's and Downings - Jones.

Plough - Tong Norton   Shaw Yard   Samuel Yates. *now burned down.*

Acorn - White Oak   Mrs. Starkie. (Brewood Perambulation) [see below]

Crown - Havannah   Mr. Bucknall.

Malt Shovel - 1 tenant only Mr. Bothams 1832-43.

1824. *Jan 16, William Moore, Bell Inn, Tong, aged 67, buried.*

1824. *Sep. 18. Sarah Moore, Bell Inn, Tong, aged 82, buried.* (She was succeeded by Thomas Radenhurst, who moved to the New Bell, Tong Norton, and then the old one was closed.)

1834. *Aug 19. Alice d. of George Bennion, Tong Norton, the Bell, Publican, bap.*

1839. *Dec 15, Jane Selena, d. of Richard Lees, Bell Inn, Tong Norton, Innkeeper, bap.*

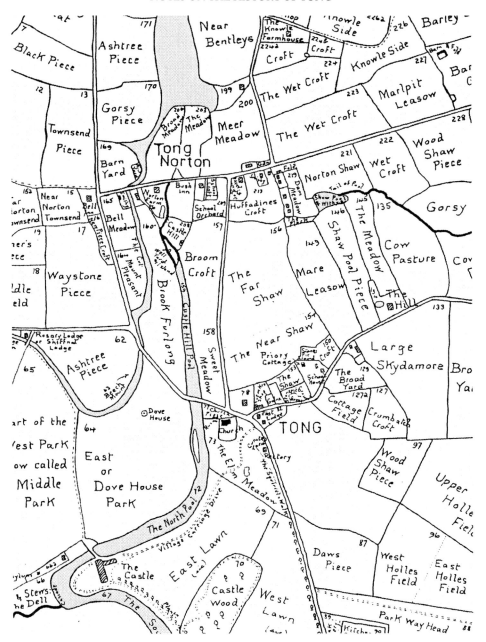

Taken from a map drawn by Mr. H D G Foxall from the Tithe map of 1855, and re-produced with permission of Shropshire Archives.

Brewood Perambulation

To the commencement of Tong near the beershop known by the name of the Royal Oak? May 25 1838.

To the shire stone at a lodge called "the Royal Oak" where those who had not previously made the perambulation were bumped. (1861).

In the catalogue of Sept. 1855, is the following:- **The Great and Small Tythes** of the entire Parish of Tong, stated to contain 3464 acres 3 roods 37 poles, have been commuted, and the Rent Charges apportioned in lieu thereof, amounting in the whole to the sum of £391. 1s. 10d. per ann., subject to the usual annual variations, having reference to the seven years previous average price of corn. The Tithe Rent Charges amounting to the sum of £25. 9s. 10d. are payable to the owner of the Tong Castle Estate, being for lands and premises not belonging to or part of the estate. The Tithe Rent Charge amounting to the above sum of £365. 12s. 0d. arises from the entire lands and premises comprising the Tong Castle Estate and also the 3 acres 1 rood 14 poles taken possession of by the Shrewsbury and Birmingham Railway Co. The sum of £10. 12s. 0d. is apportioned in respect of Tithe rent Charge on Ruckley Wood Farm containing 128 acres 3 roods 24 poles.

1855. On Tuesday September 11, 1855, the whole of the Durant property was sold by auction. The Tong portion was bought by the Right Hon. The Earl of Bradford, the Ruckley Wood Farm by Mr. John Jones, of Ruckley Grange. It was sold subject to the purchaser keeping in repair the chancel of Tong Church; also the Dam and head to the Kilsall Pool; and the Bolt Trough or Floodgate therefrom, with the cascade and weir for waste water and gates thereto. The charges on the estate were stipend paid to the clergyman £80; sum for widows' almshouses £16; sum for factory money £22. The population of the parish was then over 500, and there were scarcely any poor in it.

1856. A vestry meeting held on Oct. 23, authorised the diverting of the road leading from Weston to Wolverhampton, where it was crossed by the road leading from Tong Norton to Brewood, whereby a saving in distance of 99 yards was effected.

Tithe Apportionments for Tong
1857 Bagshaw's Gazeteer:
The following is the Tithe Apportionment for Tong.

Land Owner	Description of Premises	Quantity			Rent Charge		
		A	R	P	£	s.	d.
Earl of Bradford	Lizard Mill, House, land etc.	330	3½	10	0	3	4
Tong Castle	Stable garden and land etc.	26	0	0	7	0	0
Mr. W. Evans, of Boscobel.	Land	2	1	2	0	6	0
Parsonage	House, building, church-yard	2	0	37	0	0	0
Mr. W. Jones, of Tong Norton	Houses, gardens etc.	2	2	15		18	0
Ruckley Grange	Houses, land, woods etc.	123	3	32	17	2	6
Tong Estate	Houses, lands, woods etc.	493	0	35	25	9	10
		2971	3	2	365	12	0
	Total	3464	3	37	391	1	10

1858. A vestry meeting held on Jan. 14, authorised the churchwardens to alter the reading desk, and substitute two benches in lieu of the chairs in the belfry and the expenses attending such alterations to be defrayed out of the church rate.

1861. George John Warren, Lord Vernon, and Francis Maria Emma, his first cousin and 2nd. wife, of Sudbury Hall, Derbyshire, came here to visit the tombs of their ancestors, the eighth of October, 1861.(note in vestry book.)

1862. March 28. List of ratepayers liable to serve as Parish Officers, occupiers of Offoxey, Meesehill, Park, New Building, Tong Hall, Tong Hill Farm. Bell Inn, Lizard Mill, Ruckley Wood, Ruckley Grange, Tong Lodge, Tong Knowle, Norton Farm. (do.)

1866. April – a surplice .... £1. 5s. 0d.
In 1662 the churchwardens paid £2 .3s. 0d. for a surplice; in 1810 the price was £3. 12s. 6d; and in 1844 the new surplice cost £3. 0s. 0d.
1866: Cattle plague very bad, but not in Tong. Harvest unfinished, very wet, Oct. 13. J. W. Harding (in Burial Register.)

1867.

Jan 25	Mr Bank's Bill	10	7	10
	Mr. Hayward's Bill	3	15	4½
Sept.	Mr. Hayward's Bill	31	18	0
	Mr. Bank's Bill	2	7	0
	Huffadine's Bill	4	4	2

These all relate to work at the church. Mr. Banks was an ironmonger in Wolverhampton. He supplied new stove pipes, the price of which caused much discussion at the time. Mr. Heywood was a painter in Shifnal who cleaned and whitewashed the whole church, varnished the oak in the chancel, and removed all the ornamental inscriptions over the arches in the nave. Huffadine, the village carpenter, repaired the pews putting doors on many of them.

In November of this year Elihu Burritt paid a visit to Tong, of which he speaks in his "Walks in Black Country."

1868. A subscription was made in 1868 to augment the living of the Minister of Tong by the undernamed

Ecclesiastical Commissioners	£600
Church Extension Society	£200
Poor Benefice Fund	£100
The Right Hon. The Earl of Bradford	£227
J. Hartley, Esq.	£25
T. Thorneycroft, Esq.	£25
Orlando Bridgeman, Esq.	£5
R. Horman-Fisher, Esq.	£5
Th	£5
+e Misses George	
Miss Stockley	£4
C. Corser, Esq.	£2
G. C. Savage, Esq.	£2
Total	£1200

This was entrusted to the Ecclesiastical Commissioners so that the living is now £120 gross, viz £40 from Commissioners; £30 annuity left by Lord Pierpont; £30 in lieu of tithes left by Duke of Kingston; £40 in lieu of diet at Tong Castle, and £6 in lieu of use of stable there, and keep of horse in Park. (R. G. L.)

1869. A vestry meeting held July 29 "sanctioned a proposal made by the Earl of Bradford to stop up or divert and turn so much of a highway, being a bridle and a footway leading out of the Turnpike Road from Tong to Newport at or near a place called the Havannah towards Weston Mill and Weston under Lizard, and to give instead a similar highway being a bridle and footway already made."

1871. The Conveyance of the Tong School land to the Minister and Churchwardens of Tong is dated Dec. 30, 1871. It conveys to the Minister and Churchwardens of Tong all that piece of land on the north side of the road from Tong to the Meashill containing 870 square yards to be for ever hereafter appropriated as a school for the education of children and adults or children only of the labouring , manufacturing and other poor in the principles of the Christian Religion according to the doctrine of the Church of England, and as a residence for the teacher or teachers. To be in all respects under the management and control of the Minister and Churchwardens of the parish of Tong, or in his absence of his licensed curate, provided always that at any time hereafter the Bishop of the diocese, if he shall see fit, may with the consent of the Minister for the time being, appoint (under his hand and seal) a Committee of Management for the said school or schools in such a manner as he (the Bishop) may direct.

Tong Parochial School closed on 31ˢᵗ August 1960, and is now a private house.

The School House, the home of the schoolmaster, was built in 1874 – see under 1871. Here is an old photo of it and below a photo as it is today with its front remarkably little altered.

The houses at Tong Hill (Brazier, Millingtons etc.) were formerly occupied by an old family of Price, weavers, various articles connected with the trade were in existence in one of the rooms a few years ago. Brazier's parlour was the weaving room. It was in this house that John Baddeley, clockmaker, was born.

The village workhouse was at Tong Norton, and was kept for years by R. Tagg and his wife, who also taught the scholars there. A family named Salt also lived at it and their daughter Martha married John Shutt and had several children there. The Shutt family is said to have come from Flanders, and that the name was 'Shutz'.

The Tong Lending Library was first started by Rev. C. T. Wilson in January 1878, Mr. Inglis being the manager of it.

In 1884 a great boxing match was fought in a field behind the Bell Inn between W. Rowley and Spittle, both of Wednesbury for £30. Spittle won after 15 hard fought rounds.

The Restoration of Tong Church

1887. The Rev. G. C. Rivett-Carnac began the restoration of the church and effected a great many improvements under the guidance of Mr. Street as architect. The following is from a letter of William Darymple Maclagan, the late Archbishop of York (1891-1909), then Bishop of Lichfield (1878-1890).

> "Sept. 17, 1887. I am glad to hear of the good progress you are making in the restoration of your very fine church, and I sincerely trust that there will be no difficulty in raising a sufficient fund for so good a purpose. The church is well worthy of all the care that can be bestowed on it, and I am thankful to know that you are dealing with the matter wisely and not attempting too much."

The Restoration Committee, however, found that the undertaking was beyond their resources, and so the work was not finished till the late Earl of Bradford took the matter in hand.

The following are the notes left by the Rev. J. H. Courtney Clarke in his Church Register.

1891.

June 8   Chancel closed for restoration

June 19   Workmen opened Durant Vault in Chancel and Stanley Vault in sacrarium. The former contained 10 coffins viz. 3 illegible.

(4) Geo. Durant, B. 1776, D. 1844.

(5) Rose Durant died March 24, 1838 aged 31.

(6) Maria Durant. B. Nov. 22, 1800, died April 15, 1833.

(7) Cecil son of George Durant died March 24, 1832 aged 6 months.

(8) Belle B. Sept. 25, 1807, died Sept. 6, 1835.

(9) Mark Hanbury Durant, son of Geo. and Marianne Durant B. Nov. 5, 1808, died Aug. 22, 1815.

(10) Benjamin Charnock Payne died 14 May, 1793 age 38.

The Stanley vault contained

(1) a complete coffin of "The Right Hon. Gervas Lord Pierrepoint died May 22, 1715."

(2) the lead coffin cut open of Sir Thomas Stanley with the inscription on a lead plate "Hic jacet Thomas Stanley[98], Miles, filius secundus Edwardi comitis Darbi, maritus Margarite filie et une heredum Georgii Vernon militis, qui obiit vicessimo primo die decembris anno regni reginae Elizabeth – decimo nono; anno Domini milesimo quin-

---

[98] [Here lies Sir Thomas Stanley, Knight, second son of Edward, Earl of Derby, husband of Margaret, daughter and co-heir of George Vernon, Knight, who died on the 21st December in the 19th year of the reign of Queen Elizabeth AD 1576. God have mercy on his soul. Amen. By me John Lathom. (Translation from Griffiths p. 65)]

gentessimo septuagessimo sexto." Anima miserea-
tur Deus. Amen Per me Johannem in Lathomum[99].
(3) A lead coffin cut open and with no name on it.
(4) A square box containing remains in lime. This
box might have contained the bones of the little
son of Sir Thomas.

June 20   The old floor was found 9 in. under present floor in
the chancel, and below the arch of the Durant Vault.

June 29   Mr. Ewan Christian visited the church and decided to
raise the chancel floor over the vaults and not to fill
them up. The Willoughby slab to be removed from
the centre of the chancel between the vestry and south
door to the floor east of stalls on north side. The
screen and stalls to be raised and moved east to clear
pillars. The lead coffin on north side of Stanley vault
supposed to be Sir T. Stanley, but much broken, is in
the shape of stone coffins, and Mr. Christian considers
it much older than the other lead coffins.

June 30   In excavating the chancel floor 2 skulls, arms and
thighs were found, one beneath the other at the east
end of the north stalls, they both lay with head to
south and feet to north and were in position as originally laid. The lower one was not disturbed, the upper
one was placed in the Stanley Vault behind the oldest
coffin. The original floor 9 in. below the floor just removed, shewed the tiles laid according to the correct
pattern at the back of the stalls.

July 3   Closed Stanley Vault. Opened Willoughby Vault situ-

---

[99] In the reign of Henry the 4th Sir John Stanley (who died 1414), married Isabel the daughter and
heire of Sir Thomas Latham, who for her dowrie amongst many other lands, brought the sump-
tuose seate called Latham House, which ever since hath been the seate of the Stanleys. (Gough's
Middle p. 23.)

ated in centre of chancel between south and vestry doors, and to the east of the Durant Vault. Only one coffin in it with plate bearing the inscription "The Hon. Henry Willoughby died Dec. 3rd 1738 aged 33." The arms on the plate still retain some of the gold and blue colouring.

July 7   Removed stalls. A Maltese cross in a circle traced on the wall behind the panel above the stalls on both north and south sides. No sign of plaster on the walls.

July 8   Removed altar. The inside was of solid masonry. There was no sign of plaster or paint on the wall behind.

1892

Feb. 15   Nave of the church closed for restoration.

Feb. 20   A vault discovered in centre aisle, and under tomb of Richard and Margaret Vernon; no coffins in it. And only 3 or 4 feet deep. The arch having fallen on one side, the whole was filled up.

Feb. 22   Golden Chapel cleared out. Tomb of Arthur Vernon exposed, a slab of marble 8ft. 5in. by 4ft. 1in. with brass figure in centre, chalice and paten at the top, and arms in each corner. The old altar slab with the 5 crosses cut in the stone found in floor at east end.

Mar. 8   Platform in south-east corner of chapel proved to have been the site of the stalls. One stall end and the corner post and half a 2nd. Stall end found among the supports of pews in the church.

Mar. 22   The south screen moved back to its original place which was shewn by the hole in the south wall for the top beam of the screen, which had been covered up by a thin slab of stone, and the marks down the wall.

April 7 The Great Bell lowered through the trap in belfry ceiling, rolled on its side out of the south door and loaded upon a float at the west end of the church in the field. Height of bell 4ft. 6½ in., width at mouth 5ft. 2¼in., estimated weight 50 cwt.

April 26 It was settled to raise and repair bookcase in vestry and make a new cupboard for surplices underneath. To floor vestry with oak blocks on concrete. To increase weight of great Bell from 2 tons 1 cwt. 1 qr. present weight to 50 cwt. To turn Stanley Tomb east and west, and to repair it and other tombs. To remove organ westward to within 2 feet of north screen. To make the floor in the stall of the Vernon chantry of oak blocks.

June 10 Figures removed from top of pillars on Stanley Tomb because they did not belong there. Mr. Bridgman of Lichfield had seen similar figures on a tomb at Long Melford, Suffolk, which he thinks were designed by the same man.

June 20 Great Bell arrived from Loughborough and was taken into church by south door and placed ready for lifting. (The bill for recasting, iron frame, and guides was £230.)

June 21 Great Bell raised and put in its place.

June 23 Reopening Services. Preachers during octave Bishop of Lichfield, and Revs. E. P. Nicholas, C. J. Littleton, T. B. Lloyd, H. J. Wilkinson, W. S. Swayne, J. I. Brooks, M. H. Scott.

The great bell of Tong, weighing nearly 2 ½ tons, was raised again on 21st June 1892.

These strict rules for when the Great Bell may be rung were published on this board. The later board shows the warning notice for ringers by J. E. Auden himself, and the churchwardens.

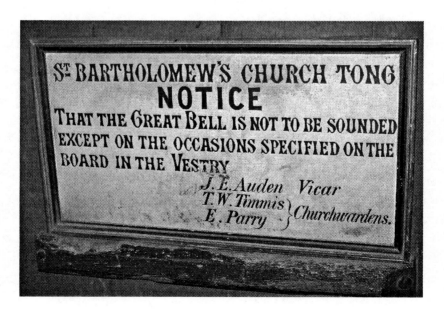

1894. July 26. The members of the Royal Archaeological Institute visited the church. Some opinions expressed by members.

1. Mr. W. H. St. John Hope M. A., Hon. Secretary Antiquarian Society, thought so-called ciborium 'a very beautiful specimen of a German drinking cup, temp. Henry VIII.'
2. Several members thought the seats were probably of date of end of 15th cent. Mr. T. J. Micklethwaite F. S. A. said that the expression 'Reforming' used in Mr. Mitton's will, 1480, the usual expression for re-seating.
3. Collegiate Churches were often divided into three, probably screen, as at present, and rood screen between nave and belfry, with people's altar in centre and a door on each side leading up to choir who wd. be under belfry.

Near the Castle at a gateway out of Dingle into Park, on each pillar was an iron harp, on one pillar a verse of T. Moore's, "The harp that once thro' Tara's halls etc.," on the other "No more to chiefs and ladies bright." These were removed, the verses and stones are now in pulpit near convent. "Fear God etc." in Greek too there. I saw the old harps lying in the wood not so very long ago.

1872. July 13 at 10 Kent Gardens, Ealing, G. C. S. Durant, late Capt. 12th Lancers in 43rd year.

1876. March 15 at St. Leonards on Sea, Lucinda, wife of G. Durant in her 68th year.

1876. March 29 at Deal, Edith, eldest d. of the late Capt. G. A. A. Durant.

1876. Oct. 1 at South Bank Terrace, Kensington, Celeste, wid. of Geo. Durant.

1908. Feb. 18 at Bournville, near Birmingham, aged 54, Edwin, 4th son of A. E. B. Durant of Gailey, Staffordshire.

1874. Ap. 10, Capt. G. H. A. Durant aged 62 (?60).

Francis Chambley of the Holt had a son Manoah, who was married at Tong.

Briefs In Tong Register

1660

May the 13th, then was Collected in the p'ish Church of Tong eight shillings & eleaven penc for *Southwold, alias Souldby* in the county of Suffolke.

August the 25th, then was collected in the parish Church of Tonge five shillings and ten penc for *Willenhall* in the county of Stafford.

1661

April the 28th day, then was collected in the parrish of Tonge foure shillings towards the releefe of *John Davis* & others, his sade participates whose habitations were in the county of Hereford but were burnt & consumed & they exposed to great penury.

Collected in the p'ish of Tonge (June the second one thousand six hundred & sixty one) five shillings towards the releefe of the Inhabitants of the Towne of *Elmely Castle* in the county of Worcester.

Collected in the Church of Tonge ye 14th of July 1661 towards ye releefe of the towne of *Ilminster* in ye county of Somerset five shillings.

Collected in ye said Church of Tong seven shillings towards ye releefe of ye city of *Oxford*: it was collected ye 4th day of Augt. 1661.

Collected in the Church of Tonge the 18th day of Augst: 61 the sume of 3s. 2d. towards ye relefe of *James Mulnill Esqre*. late of Clanough in ye county of Downe in ye Realme of Ireland.

Collect: in ye parrish of Tong foure shillings two pens: for ye releefe of *Quatt* in ye county of Sallop.

Collect: in ye parrish of Tong three shillings six pens towards ye releefe of ye Destressed inhabitants of *Motheringham* in ye Lincolnesshire.

Collect: in ye parrish of Tonge ten shillings two pens towards ye repaire of *Condover Church.*

Collect: in the parrish of Tong two shillings two pens for ye releefe of ye towne of *Watchett* in the county of Somersett.

Co'ct in ye parrish of Tong ye sume of five shillings towards ye releefe of ye inhabitants of *Bridgnorth.*

Collect: in ye parrish of Tong two shillings six pens towards ye releefe of *Hen. Harison, Marrinor.*

Collect: [June 1, 1662] in ye parish 14s. 11d. towards ye releefe of *Elianor, of Langullo,* in ye county of Radnor.

Collect: in ye parrish of Tonge 15s. 6d. towards ye releefe of *Drayton Magna.*

Collected ye 8th day of December in ye church of Tonge 2s. 10d. towards ye releefe of ye *Protestant Churches in ye Dukedome of Lithuania,* John de Kraine Krainskey Petitioner 1661.

1662
Coll: in ye parish Church of Tonge the summe of [blank] towards ye releefe of partys inhabiting in *Walton of ye Club* in ye parish of Ercll Magna in ye county of Sallop.

1663
Collected in ye parrish of Tong at ye request of the inhabitants of *Sheriffhales* towards ye releefe of those yt suffered fire there £3 14s. 4.

Coll: in ye parish church of Tong upon ye 9th day of September in ye yeare 1663 the sume of 9s. towards ye releefe of ye inhabitants of *Cherington* in ye county of Sallop.

Coll: the sume of 3s. 9d. in the parrish church of Tong for & towards the releefe of the inhabitants of the towne of *Hexham* in the county of Northumberland January ye 31.

Collect: in the Church of Tong towards ye repaire of *Basing Church* in the county of Southampton, the sume of 4s. 3d. August ye 28th, 1664.

1664
Collect: in ye Church of Tong ye sume of 2s. 2d. towards ye repayre of ye p'ish Church in *Chester: Sept. 25.*

Coll: in the Church of Tong in Novemb. for & towards ye repaire of the Church of *Croomey (Cromer?) alias Shipden* 2s. 4d.

Coll: in the Church of Tong the sume of 2s. 0d. towards the repaire of ye Church of *Pytheham* in ye county of Sussex December the 4th.

Coll: in ye Church of Tong December 18th for & towards the repaire of the bridge in the p'ish of *Trapson* [Thrapston?] in the county of Northampton.

Coll: in the Church of Tong Jan. 8th the summe of 2s. 0d. for and towards the repaire of *Tinmouth* Church in the county of Northumberland.

Coll: in the Church of Tong 2s. 11d. for and towards the repaire of the Church of *Lidney* in the county of Gloucester Jan. 29th.

1665

Coll: in the p'ish Church of Tong the summe of 2s. 3d. Aprill ye 2nd, for one *Shuter, a tanner of Tamworth* in Warwickshire.

Collect: in the p'ish Church of Tong the sume of 2s. 4d. towards the repaire of ye Church of *Lymington* in ye county of Southampton, May the 14.

Collect: in ye p'ish Church of Tong the sume of 2s. 6d. for ye fire at *Cockshutt* in ye county of Sallop, July the 2nd.

Coll: in the Church of Tong the summe of two shillings towards ye releefe of the poore inhabitants of *Bidford,* in the county of Warwick. July 23.

Collect: in the Church of Tong the summe of two shillings and nine pens for *David Long of Norrington* in the county of Wilts, June ye 18th.

Coll: in ye Church of Tonge, March 11th, 2s. 7d. for & towards ye reliefe of ye inhabitants of *fflookeburgh* in ye county of Lancaster.

Collected this 17th day of June, Anno Dom.1666, in the parrish Church of Tong by the churchwardens, the summe of two shillings five pence for ye reliefe of *Ann Toms of War:* widowe.

There was collected the 22nd of July, Anno Dom, 1666, at the parrish Church of Tongue in the county of Sallop, the sume of 1s. 10d. by the churchwardens, for the repaire of the Church of *Warburrow* in the countie of Oxford.

Collected the 24th of ffeb: 1666, for the Towne of *Worksop* in the county of Nottingham who recd. a great losse by ffire, in ye Church of Tonge in ye county of Sallop, the summe of two shillings seaven pence.

Collected June the 16th, Anno 1667, for the towne of *Pool* in the countie of Mountgomeroie (the summe of two shillings 3 pence) whoe recevd a great losse by fire.

Collected by the Churchwardens towards the losse of *Newport* by fire, the summe of 20 s. this 6th of October, 1667.

Collected at the parish Church of Tonge, by the churchwardens, for *Loburroah* [Loughborough?] in ye countie of Leicester, this 29 of December Anno 1667, the summe of Two shillings and 11d.

1668

The Inhabitants of the p'ish of Tong, Doe aknoledg to have recd.
    an aquittance from
 Mr. Edward Bird of twentie three shill: collected for sufferers by
    fire in London: the 11th of January, 1668.

Collected in the parish Church of Tonge, in ye county of Sallop, this last of October, Anno 1669, the summe of 7s. and 4d. by us Robert Woer and Robert Blockley, churchwardens: this collection was for ye towne of *Meole Brace* in ye county of Sallop.

Collected at ye Church of Tonge, in the countie of Sallop, Aprill this 3rd anno Dom. 1670, ye summe of 3s. 6d, by Robert Woer and Robert Blockley, churchwardens.

Collected at ye Church of Tonge for ye towne of *Beckles*, in ye county of Suffolke, Sept. 18, 1670, ye summe of three shillings by William Cope and Robert Blakemore, churchwardens.

Collected at ye Church of Tonge, for ye towne of *Iseleham* in ye county of Cambridge, Sept. ye 11th, 1670, ye summe of three shillings, by Wm. Cope and Robert Blakemore, churchwardens.

Collected at Tonge church, Jan. 4, 1673, the summe of ffive shillings six pence by Wm. Norton & John Smith, churchwardens for *St. Katherin neare ye Tower in London.*

Collected at Tong Church, March 22nd, 1673, the summe of three shillings six pence by Wm. Norton & John Smith, churchwardens, for *St. Margarets at Cliffe in ye countie of Kent.*

The following are entered in the old Churchwardens' Account Book:-

June 17, 1674. Collected for Thomas Wakesring of Black Halse, in ye parish of Wolverhampton in ye county of Stafford ye summe of three shillings six pence.

Aug. 30, 1674. collected for Denigall in Ireland the summe of ffoure shillings.

March 14, 1674(5). Collected for Nether Wellop in ye county of Southampton ye summe of 5s. 3d.

April 4, 1675. Collected for the parish church of Benenden in ye county of Kent ye summe of 5s. 3d.

April 11, 1675. Collected for Redborne in ye county of Hertford ye summe of 3s. 8d.

June 6, 1675. Collected for Walton in ye countie of Norfolk ye summe of 3s. 7d.

Ffeb. 4, 1676. Collected for Eaton in Bucks the summe of foure shillings.

Nov. 25, 1676. Collected for Northampton the summe of 1 li. 4s. 10d.

April 15, 1677. Collected for Cottenham in Cambridgeshire, the summe of six shillings.

May 7, 1677. Collected for Towchester, Northamptonshire, the summe of three shillings tenn pence.

---- 1680. Collected towards ye Redemption of some Christians taken in Turkish slavery ye sum of one pound six shillings and nine pence.

---- 1680. Collected for ye ffire att East Derham ye sum of ffive shillings & eight pence.

(No date)? 1670. For the Breife Granted towards the Redemption of the poore captives Fez and Morocco the sum of 13s. 9d.

Receipts for the following as well as many already quoted are still preserved in the Tong Chest:-

March ye 20th, 1661. Receaved then of the Minister of Tonge two shillings six pens being mony collected Upon the Sumons of A lett'r patent granted by his Ma'ty Unto me: I say received by me Edward Strichly his Marke.

The twentye fiust of maye 1673. Then recd. from the hands of William Scott of Tong Norton in the countie of Sollop the sume of Eleaven shillings which was collected in the p'ish of Tonge for Tibberton by reason of theire losse by fire in the yeare of the Raigne of the Kinge that now is.

Oct. 17, 1706. Ye Iniskilling breif 15s. 6d.

Oct. 24, 1706. Terington 1s. 9d; Darlington 7s. 4d; Morgansland 6s. 2d; Chattriss 2s. 1d; Ballford 1s. 9d.

May 2, 1707. Towcester Brief 2s. 7d; Northmarson Brief 2s. 4d.

April 28, 1710. Mittan 9s. 1¾d.

Oct. 17, 1710. Chalfont 3s. 6½d; Ashton 6s. 1d; Stockton 6s. 1d;
Northfleet 2s. 3½d; Rotherith 2s. 9½.

June 1, 1711. Eusham 5s. 10d; Paningham 2s. 10d; Twyford 4s.
2d; Cardigan 3s. 11d; Cockermouth 6s. 7½ ; Colchester 4s. 5d;
Wishard 2s. 6d; Ide 3s. 7d. Rotherich Church 3s. 11d.
July 25, 1711. Eddinburgh 2s. 10d; St. Hellens 2s. 3d.

October 29, 1713. Woodham 7s. 1½d;   Warmingham   2s. 5d;
Southwell 12s. 2d; Burton 12s. 5d; Rudgeley 6s. 7d; Adams 6d.

June 25, 1714. St. Margets 2s. 2d; St. Maries 2s. 6d.; Leighton 2s.
3d; Shipwash 2s.0d; Wytheridge 2s. 0d.; Quatford 2s. 9½d.

Oct. 28, 1714. St John Baptist 1s. 11d; Burslam Church 2s.3d;
Blandfford 5s. 7d; Bottisham 5s. 2d; Dorsester 2s. 2d.

May 6, 1715. Bowyer 4s.1d;   Derby 4s. 9d;   Warwick 5s. 4d;
Torksey 2s. 4d; Shoreham 2s. 1d; Ruthin 4s.7d.

Oct. 27, 1715. Dryneton 2s. 4d; Kentford 2s. 1d; Blymhill 4s. 8d;
St. Peters [Chester] 2s. 5d; Cowkeeper 10s. 4d; Newcastle 4s.
11d.

April 19, 1716. Sunderland New Church 2s. 3d.

April 19, 1716. Wrexham 1s 11d; Lerpoole 2s.1d; Mitcham 1s.
8½d; St. Maries (Lichfield) 4s. 4d.

Oct. 4, 1716. Spallding 8s. 9d; Upton 2s. 2d; Temstwood 7s. 6d;
Aaron 2s. 7½d; Burton 1s. 4½d.

Oct. 31, 1718. Cherrington 1s. 7d; Newland 1s. 10d; Newington
1s. 10d; Ashburne 2s. 3d; Penrith 2s.1d, Grindon 2s.1d.

Parish clerks of Tong

Thomas Mayer, Clarke of the Parish, buried Feb. 22, 1655.

Humphrey Mayer, buried April 1661.

Thomas Harrison was made clerk April 29, 1661. Buried April 17, 1683.

George Harrison. Buried May 3, 1711.

Michael Ore, parish clerk, buried April 4, 1785.

Robert Ore. In the recess in the N. wall of the chancel, when it was opened in 1900, was found written "Robert Ore is clerk at Tong Church", and the date March 19, 1790. Robert Ore, Tong Knowle, aged 71, was buried Aug. 2, 1826.

Robert Tagg 1807.

Andrew Cousins, Clerk of this Parish, Free School House, Tong Hill, aged 71,was buried Oct. 25, 1829. Was acting clerk 1813.

William Woolley, clockmaker, Tong Hill, buried Dec. 10, 1856, aged 74.

Richard Machesney, Tong Hill, aged 53, was buried Feb. 17, 1846.

John Wood. Resigned on leaving the parish, 1851.

John Longstaff. Resigned on leaving the parish 1871.

John Boden, Tong, aged 72, for 42 years Postmaster, and 22 years clerk of this Parish, buried Feb. 24, 1893.

George Henry Boden, now *[1913 at the latest]* Postmaster and Clerk, having succeeded his father in both offices.

(William Woolley was discharged from his office as parish clerk, because he called a preacher from Bridgnorth, who complained that there was no mirror in the vestry, a "confounded coxcomb". The present mirror was given by Mr. Durant owing to the above incident.)

Churchwardens of Tong 1630 – 1908

??Probably Tong	??Probably Tong Norton
1630 Roger Austen of Ruckley Grange. Buried July 6, 1648.	Thomas Halfpenye. Buried May 2, 1635.
1631 Thomas Lateward, gent. Buried Jan. 14, 1636-7.	Name lost.
1632 Thomas Scot, of Tong Norton. Buried May 14, 1671-2.	Name lost.
1634 John Baddyley. Buried May 9, 1671.	Thomas Painton. Buried Feb. 11, 1641-2.
1635 George Salter, gent. Buried March 12, 1641-2.	Thomas Clarke. Buried Aug. 13, 1647.
1636 George Salter	Thomas Clarke
1637 Thomas Scot (also 1632)	Thomas Holmes. Buried Dec. 8, 1650.
1638 Morris Yeavans, of Tong Norton. Buried June 17, 1663.	Thomas Earle, of Tong. Buried Aug. 12, 1652.
1639 Morris Yeavans	Thomas Earle
1640 Ralph Homes. Buried Dec. 10, 1644.	John Cooke, of Tong. Buried June 30, 1652.
1641 Edward Bishton. Buried Feb. 17, 1648-9.	Name lost.
1642 Edward Bishton	John Poole, of the Stile. Buried June 17, 1662.
1643 Edward Bishton	John Poole
1644 Edward Bishton	John Poole
1645 Edward Bishton	John Poole
1646 Edward Bishton	John Poole
1647 Roger Austen (also 1630)	William Norton of Lizard Mill, Buried July 17, 1682.

1648	Humphrey Earle Buried Feb. 17, 1671-2.	Thomas Scot. (also 1632 and 37)
1649	Robert Burd (?)	Name lost.
1650	Robert Homes. Buried Feb. 14, 1670-71	John Cawdwell
1651	John Baddely (also 1634)	Robert Clarke
1652	Thomas Onnions of Tong. Buried July 14, 1653.	Robert Blockley, of Tong Norton. Buried Sept. 3, 1688.
1653	Thomas Harrison. Buried April 17, 1683.	William Hardwicke, for Tong Norton. Buried Feb. 23, 1676-7.
1654	Thomas Scott jun. Buried March 29, 1698.	George Holmes, Buried May 19, 1672.
1655	Robert Owen. Buried Dec. 6, 1674.	Name lost.
1656	John Bennett. Buried April 16, 1667.	William Blakemore, for Tong Norton. Buried Oct. 16, 1667.
1657	Edward Poole Buried Nov. 20, 1705.	George Meeson. Buried Jan. 24, 1682-3.
1658	William Coape	Thomas Martin. Buried Feb. 2, 1669-70
1659	William Norton of Lizard Mill. (also 1647)	John Smith of Ruckley Grange. Buried May 10, 1679.
1660	Thomas Scott (also 1654)	Humphrey Earle (also 1648)
1661	Richard Ford. Buried April 5, 1684.	Martin Wheeler. Buried April 19, 1700.
1662	Humphrey Earle (also 1648)	William Scott of Tong Norton, gent. Buried Mar. 27, 1694.
1663	William Salter	Edward Homes of Tong. Buried July 16, 1665.
1664	Robert Homes	Robert Blockley of Tong

		Norton, yeoman. Buried Sept. 3, 1688.
1665	John Baddeley, sen.	John Cooper. Buried Jan. 31, 1699-1700.
1666	Edward Bird of the Talbot Inn.	Robert Clarke, elected but did not serve.
1667	Thomas Harrison of Tong, yeoman.	Robert Blockley (for William Hardwick).
1668	George Homes	Robert Blockley (for Robert Forster, gent.)
1669	Robert Woer, of Norton, husbandman, (also 1655)	John Evans. Buried May 30, 1702.
1670	William Cope of Tong, husbandman	Robert Blakemore
1671	Wiliam Cope	Thomas Harrison (for Francis Homes for Tong Norton)
1672	George Meeson of Tong, innholder (also 1657)	William Blakemore of Tong, wheelwright (for Thomas Paynton of Norton).
1673	John Smith of Ruckley Grange (also 1659)	William Norton (also 1659)
1674	Edward Poole (also 1657)	Robert Blockley of Tong Norton (for Elizabeth Martin[100] widow of Tong Norton.)
1675	Francis Homes. Buried Dec. 24, 1720.	Thomas Harris (for Tong Norton)
1676	Thomas Lateward of Tong, gent. Buried Oct 4 1685	William Scott (also 1662)

---

[100] Elizabeth Martin (1674) was connected with the escape of the king in 1657. Elizabeth, the wife of Bartholomew Martin, was buried at White Ladies cemetery in January, 1707. Bartholomew Martin was a "serving boy" in White Ladies House in 1657, and was sent to Boscobel to fetch William Pendrill directly the king arrived there. (cf Flight of the King p.20). She and her husband were R. C. 'recusants.'

1677	Richard Ford (also 1661)	Martin Wheeler (also 1661)
1678	William Salter	William Scott for Tong Norton (also 1662, 1676)
1679	Nathaniel Myveart	Robert Blockley
1680	Francis Homes (also 1675)	Robert Blockley
1681	John Baddeley	John Cope. Buried Oct. 8, 1707
1682	Ralph Adeney	?? (for Avis Clarke, widow[101]).
1683	John Homes	Richard Pool. Buried Nov.1, 1706
1684	George Harrison	Robert Blockley
1685	Thomas Owen	John Evans (also 1669)
1686	Robert Blakemore	Robert Scholey. Buried July 10, 1728.
1687	Roger Roden of Ruckley, yeoman. Buried Feb. 17, 1704-5.	Robert Homes, husband-man. Buried July 21, 1728.
1690	Charles Lateward	Roger Mason. Buried Nov. 5, 1728.
1691	Thomas Scott	Richard Marion.
1692	William Salter, gent.	Martin Wheeler, yeoman. (also 1661,1677)
1693	William Salter	Name lost.
1695	Fenihouse Lees, of Tong, yeoman.	John Hamnet, of Tong Norton, yeoman.
1696	Fenihouse Lees	John Hamnet
1697	John Fox, of Lyzard	John Blockley

---

[101] 1682. Her descendant, Mr. J. H. Clarke, had a copy of De Civitate Dei in black letter, bound in thick leather, and in it the name of Avise Clearke, Lizard Graunge. It was printed at Antwerp and at the end of the vol, cut to fill it when binding were several pages cut from some religious works, missals and the like. The illuminations were all done by hand, and the capitals were glorious, the colours as fresh as if they had only just been done, one fragment contained remarks on Holy Matrimony. It was presented to an R. C. priest. Avise Clarke was probably the widow of Robert C. of 1666.

Grange.
Buried Sept. 6, 1735.

1698	Thomas Pemberton, yeoman.	George Harrison.
1699	Thomas Ore, jun. of Tong.	George Parker, of Tong Norton, husbandman.
1701	Robert Scholey (also 1686)	Thomas Smith. Buried Dec. 18, 1709.
1706	Thomas Pemberton jun.	Roger Mason (also 1690)
1708	Thomas Scott of Ruckley Wood (also 1691)	Richard Beech, blacksmith. Buried Dec. 26, 1734.
1713	John Cotton, of Norton, yeoman. Buried March 24, 1732-3.	George Homes, husbandman.
1715	Thomas Ore (also 1699)	George Parker (also 1699)
1714	John Reynolds. Buried April 14, 1719.	Thomas Blakemore
1716	Ralph Roden of Ruckley, husbandman.	Name lost
1717	John Cotton of Norton, yeoman (also 1713)	John Pemberton, yeoman.
1718	William Harris	William Whistons
1719	Thomas Woodshaw, yeoman.	Thomas Paynton, yeoman.
1721	Thomas Woodshaw	Name lost
1723	William Harris (also 1718)	Name lost
1726	Richard Duncalfe, cooper. Buried Jan. 2, 1737-8.	Richard Marrian
1727	George Homes	Robert Ore
1729	Thomas Wright, yeoman.	Richard Evans, yeoman.
1730	John Marrion	John Poole, of Meosell.
1731	Thomas Ore	John Baddeley
1732	George Parker, of Norton, husbandman. (also 1699)	William Blakemore, cordwainer.
1733	Walter Clay, of Hubbal,	John Pickin of Tong.

husbandman. Buried May 7, 1741.

Buried July 12, 1765.

1734	Walter Clay	Thomas Fox, yeoman. Buried Nov. 6, 1765.
1735	John Scholey	Walter Wheeler, of the Knowle, husbandman. Bur. April 14, 1742.
1736	William Ore	Richard Marrian
1737	George Dickenson, yeoman. Buried May 27, 1754.	John Carpenter, husbandman.
1738	John Roden, gent, Ruckley.	Richard Marrian, deputy ch.warden.
1739	Thomas Wright	John Duncalf, cooper. Buried May 4, 1778.
1740	Richard Evans of Hubbal.	John Marrian
1741	Richard Evans	William Tildesley, yeoman. Buried March 27, 1754.
1742	Richard Evans	William Tildesley
1743	George Baddeley	William Tildesley
1744	Thomas Fox, Lizard Grange.(also 1734)	Joseph Phillips, butcher. Buried June 2, 1788.
1745	John Picken	Joseph Phillips
1746	John Picken	Joseph Phillips
1747	Richard Marrion. Buried May 31, 1770.	Reginald Clay. Buried Feb. 18, 1788.
1748	Richard Marrion.	Reginald Clay.
1749	William Blakemore of the North Farm, Tong, farmer.	Name lost.
1750	William Blakemore.	Name lost.
1751	William Ore.	Name lost.
1752	William Ore.	Thomas Wheeler. Buried May 28, 1759.
1753	George Dickenson (also	John Roden (also 1738)

1737)

1754	John Duncalf (also 1739)	Name lost.
1755	John Duncalf	Name lost.
1757	George Baddeley (also 1743)	John Rowley.
1758	Thomas Fox (also 1734, 44)	Richard Darley.
1759	William Barker	Joseph Phillips
1760	William Barker	Joseph Phillips.
1761	William Blakemore	Name lost.
1762	William Blakemore	Name lost.
1763	Edward Wright. Buried Nov. 3, 1769.	Name lost
1764	George Steventon	Name lost.
1766	William Blakemore	John Roden
1767	John Stubbs, Meesehill. Buried Aug. 12, 1817, aged 87.	Richard Ward, Tong Hill, yeoman.
1768	Thomas Ore, clockmaker	George Stubbs
1769	William Blakemore	John Tildesley
1770	William Barker	John Stubbs (also 1767)
1771	William Darley	John Stubbs
1779	William Barker of Tong Norton, gentleman.	Name lost
1783	Thomas Rowley. Buried Nov. 6, 1813, aged 70.	Richard Marrion
1785	John Stubbs, farmer (also 1767)	John Morris
1789	Francis Chambley, Holt Farm.	John Morris
1792	John Stubbs	Thomas Andrews
1796	Thomas Andrews, of Tong Park.	William Lowe.
1797	John Clarke	Richard Phillips
1798	John Stubbs	Thomas Andrews

1799	John Ward	Thomas Rowley
1800	James Jones, Tong Norton, schoolmaster. (1797)	John Duncalfe
1801	Richard Phillips	James Jones
1802	William Chesher Glover, Lizard Grange, gentleman.	James Jones, Tong Norton. Buried March 29, 1834, aged 76.
1803	Richard Phillips	James Jones
1804	Edward Phillips, Tong.	John Stubbs
1805	Thomas Rowley (also 1783)	John Stubbs
1806	John Ward, Tong Park.	John Titley, Ruckley.
1807	William Lowe	Edward Phillips
1808	John Titley	James Jones
1809	Edward Phillips	Benjamin Yardley
1810	Edward Phillips	John Stubbs
1811	James Jones	Edward Phillips
1812	James Jones	John Titley, Ruckley Wood, farmer.
1813	James Jones	Francis Weaver, Lizard Mill. Buried June 27, 1842, aged 76.
1814	James Jones (now described as malster.)	Francis Weaver, miller.
1815	James Jones	Francis Weaver
1816	Edward Phillips	Francis Weaver
1817	Edward Phillips	Francis Weaver
1818	Edward Phillips	Francis Weaver
1819	William Lowe, Tong Norton Farm. Buried Sept. 29, 1830, aged 60.	Francis Weaver
1820	William Lowe	Francis Weaver
1821	William Lowe	Thomas Moore, Tong, farmer. Buried Jan. 11, 1871 aged 78.

1822	William Lowe	Thomas Clews, Red House, Tong, malster.
1823	Thomas Clews, seedsman	William Lowe
1824	Thomas Clews	Francis Weaver
1825	John Broughall, Tong Park.	Francis Weaver
1826	John Broughall	Francis Weaver
1827	John Broughall	Francis Weaver
1828	Robert Joynson, the Holt	Francis Weaver
1829	Robert Joynson	Francis Weaver
1830	Robert Joynson	Francis Weaver
1831	Joseph Icke, Knowle Farm.	Francis Weaver
1832	Joseph Icke	Francis Weaver
1833	William Earp, Lizard Grange, farmer.	John Broughall, Knowle Farm, farmer.
1834	William Earp	John Broughall
1835	William Earp	Thomas Icke. Tong Farm
1836	Thomas Icke, Tong Farm (now Church House), afterwards of Sydnal, died 16 March, 1858, aged 63, bur. at Sheriffhales.	William Earp
1837	Thomas Icke	William Earp
1838	Thomas Icke	William Earp
1839	Thomas Icke	Thomas Picken, Tong Hill.
1840	John Holding, White Oak.	Thomas Picken
1841	George Hempenstall[102], bailiff to Mr. Durant. Buried Nov. 30, 1859, aged 84.	Thomas Picken,
1842	Owen Bennion, Tong Hill. Buried Dec. 30, 1873, aged 80.	Abraham Hounsom, Norton Cottage, farmer.

[102] 1841 George Hempenstall was "for 50 years and 7 months a faithful servant in the family of the Durants of Tong Castle." (on gravestone)

1843	Owen Bennion	Richard Weaver, Lizard Mill.
1844	Owen Bennion	Richard Weaver
1845	Owen Bennion	Samuel Walley, Meesehill
1846	Owen Bennion	Samuel Walley
1847	Owen Bennion	Samuel Walley
1848	Owen Bennion	Samuel Walley
1849	Owen Bennion	Samuel Walley
1850	Owen Bennion	Samuel Walley
1851	Owen Bennion	Gilbert Cole Savage, Knowle Farm. Died at Orslow Dec. 19, 1884, aged 77.
1852	Owen Bennion	G. C. Savage
1853	Owen Bennion	G. C. Savage
1854	Owen Bennion	G. C. Savage
1855	Thomas Milner[103], Tong Hall. Buried March 6, 1899 aged 82.	G. C. Savage
1856	Walter Bamford, Offoxey.	G. C. Savage
1857	Walter Bamford	G. C. Savage
1858	Gilbert Cole Savage	William Worrall, New Buildings. Buried Jan. 29, 1867 aged 57.
1859	Henry Bloxham, Lizard Mill. Buried Sept. 17, 1873 aged 66.	William Worrall, yeoman.
1860	G. C. Savage	Roger Horman-Fisher[104], Tong Priory, Barrister at Law, Capt. 1st V. B. S. Stafford Regt.

[103] Mr. Milner served with the Shropshire Yeomanry in the suppression of the Chartist riots at Newtown in 1838.
[104] 1860 Mr. R. H. Fisher matriculated at Christ Church, Oxford May 15, 1839, aged 19, and was called to the Bar at the Middle Temple 1845. He was a member of the family of Fisher of St. Edith's, Wiltshire – his mother being a titled personage.

1861	G. C. Savage	R. H. Fisher
1862	G. C. Savage	R. H. Fisher
1863	G. C. Savage	R. H. Fisher
1863	G. C. Savage	R. H. Fisher
1864	G. C. Savage	R. H. Fisher
1865	G. C. Savage	R. H. Fisher
1866	G. C. Savage	R. H. Fisher
1866	G. C. Savage	R. H. Fisher
1867	G. C. Savage	R. H. Fisher
1868	G. C. Savage	Thomas Milner
1869	G. C. Savage	Thomas Milner
1870	G. C. Savage	Thomas Milner
1871	G. C. Savage	R. H. Fisher
1872	Thomas Milner	R. H. Fisher
1873	John Edwards, Park Farm.	Richard Edwards, Tong Farm (called by him Church House)
1874	Richard Edwards[105]	George Newdigate[106], West Lodge, Major Derby Militia. Died April 11, 1910 aged 85.
1875	Hugh Hunter, Offoxey.	William Davies, Tong Park. Buried Nov. 25, 1890 aged 57.
1876	Hugh Hunter	William Davies
1877	Hugh Hunter	William Davies
1878	Hugh Hunter	William Davies
1879	Thomas Sillitoe, Lizard Grange	William Davies
1880	Thomas Sillitoe	William Davies

---

[105] 1873 The Vicar nominated Mr. Baker Boulton, of Lizard Farm, as his warden at the Easter Vestry, but the Ven. Archdeacon Allen refused to admit him, as he was neither a ratepayer nor resident in the parish. On June 3rd therefore the Rev. R. G. Lawrence appointed Mr. Richard Edwards in place of Mr. Boulton.

[106] Newspaper cutting - April 1910. NEWDIGATE:- On the 11th inst., at 68, Regency Square, Brighton, George Newdigate, born 1825. fifth son of the late Francis and Lady Barbara Newdigate, formerly Lieut. Colonel of the 5th Batt. Derbyshire Regiment.

1881	Thomas Sillitoe	William Davies
1882	Thomas Sillitoe	William Davies
1883	Thomas Wall Timmis, Meesehill.	Thomas Milner
1884	T. W. Timmis . died 1910 aged 57	Thomas Milner
1885	T. W. Timmis	Thomas Milner
1886	T. W. Timmis	Thomas Milner
1887	T. W. Timmis	Thomas Milner
1888	T. W. Timmis	Thomas Milner
1889	T. W. Timmis	Thomas Milner
1890	T. W. Timmis	Thomas Milner
1891	T. W. Timmis	Thomas Milner
1892	T. W. Timmis	Thomas Milner jun.
1893	George Frederick Norton, Knowle Farm.	Thomas Milner jun.
1894	G. F. Norton, Clerk of Works to Earl of Bradford.	Thomas Milner jun.
1895	G. F. Norton	Thomas Wall Timmis
1896	Thomas Wall Timmis	Edward Parry, Tong Park.
1897	T. W. Timmis	Edward Parry
1898	T. W. Timmis	Edward Parry
1899	T. W. Timmis	Edward Parry
1900	T. W. Timmis	Edward Parry
1901	T. W. Timmis	Edward Parry
1902	T. W. Timmis	Edward Parry
1903	T. W. Timmis	Edward Parry
1904	T. W. Timmis	Edward Parry
1908	Edward Parry	Henry Bennion

Clergy in Tong

John Auden did not provide a list of Clergy, but from what he did write and from other sources, here is as accurate a list as we can make. The early years of the Church are not well documented and there are various 'lists'. The first recorded priest was Ernulf (1188-1194); possibly from 1215-1220 Robert de Shireford; 1255 William --.

Before there was a college the parish was served by monks from Shrewsbury Abbey. When in 1410 the College was founded by Isabella de Pembrugge the Warden acted as the priest of the parish. Robert Jeffery has supplied us with the following list of Wardens.

1410	William Shaw or William Moss
1411-13	William Galley
1413-18	William Mosse
1418-23	William Admondeston
1423-37	Walter Battell
1437-79	Sir Richard Eyton
1479-90	Thomas Hynkley
1490-93	John Bryken
1493-96	Thomas Brown
1496-1508	John Lygh – also Vicar of Idsall
1508	Thomas Cantrell
1515	Thomas Forster
1526-1535	Henry Bullock
1535-36	Thomas Pawson

After the Reformation the Minister of Tong appears to have become a Domestic Chaplain at the Castle. A New Vicarage was built in 1725. The following Clergy can be traced from 1602.

1602-1641 **George Meeson** *Described in an Elizabethan clergy list as 'no preacher, no degree'. See*

Vol. 1

1641-1650	**William Southall**	*See Vol. 1*
1650-1660	**Robert Hilton**	*See Vol. 1*
1660-1666	**Joseph Bradley**	*See Vol. 1*
1666-1678	**Richard Ward**	*See Vol. 1*
1679-1686	**William Cotton**	*See Vol. 1*
1686-1695	**John Hulton**	*See Vol. 1*
1695-1745	**Lewis Peitier**	*See Vol. 1*
1745-1765	**Thomas Hall**	*Curate 1730-45, See Vol. 1*
1765-1770	**Scrope Berdmore**	*See Vol. 1*
1770-1791	**Theophilus Buck-eridge**	*Curate 1765-1770.* *also Master of St. John's Hospital Lichfield.* *See Vol. 1*
1791-1807	**Charles Buckeridge**	*Curate 1781-91.Later Archdeacon of Coventry. Buried in Tong vestry. Vol. 1*
1807-1839	**John Muckleston**	*Prebendary of Lichfield,* *See Vol. 1*
1839-1843	**Leonard Henry St. George**	*See Vol. 1*
!843-1855	**George Harding**	*Also Vicar of Cheswardine. See Vol. 1*
1855-1870	**John Harding**	*See Vol. 1*
1870-1876	**Richard Lawrence**	*See Vol. 1*
1877-1882	**Charles Wilson**	*See Vol. 1*
1882-1890	**George Rivett-Carnac**	*See Vol. 1*
1890-1896	**John Henry Court-ney-Clarke**	*See Vol. 1*
1896-1913	**John Auden**	*See his biography on page 213.*
1913-1920	**W. Millington**	
1920-1926	**F. A. A. W. Heaton**	
1926-1935	**A. R. H. Guiness**	
1935-1939	**W. F. Grove**	
1939-1945	**W. H. Holdgate**	

1945-1954	**E. J. Gargery**	
1954-1956	**J. C. West**	
1956-1961	**Brian Skelding**	
1961-1971	**Leslie Yates**	
1971-1974	**John Spencer**	*Priest –in-Charge. Prebendary of Lichfield*
1974-1976	**Henry Follis**	*Priest-in-Charge. Also Rector of Blymhill*
1976-1977	**Graham Johnson**	*Priest-in-Charge and Diocesan Youth Officer*
1978-1987	**Robert Jeffery**	*from 1980 Archdeacon of Salop later Dean of Worcester*
1987-1998	**George Frost**	*Archdeacon of Salop later Archdeacon of Lichfield*
1998-	**John Hall**	*Archdeacon of Salop*

Some information about curates is given in Vol. 1
From 1983-88 Brian Turnbull was Honorary curate.

Bibliography
(as supplied by John Auden)

Carlyle	*Cromwell's Letters*
Cranage, Rev. D.H.S.	*Churches of Shropshire*
Duncan	*History of the Royal Regiment of Artillery*
Fea, Alan	*Flight of the King*
Griffiths G.	*History of Tong and Boscobel*
Hughes	*Boscobel Tracts*
O. & B.	*Owen and Blakeway: The History of Shrewsbury.*
S.A.S.T.	*Transactions of the Shropshire Archaeological Society*
	Mercurius Aulicus
	Iter Carolinum
	The Gentleman's Magazine

Biography

John. E. Auden

The Reverend John Ernest Auden was Vicar of Tong in Shropshire from 1896-1913.

A son of the Vicar of Horninglow, Auden was born at Silverdale in Staffordshire, on 13th December 1860. He was educated at Shrewsbury and Lincoln College, Oxford, taking his B. A. in 1883 and M.A. in 1887. He was ordained in the Winchester Diocese in 1883, becoming Curate of Carisbrooke with St Nicholas-in-the-Castle, Isle of Wight, 1883-5. His second curacy was Wooburn in Buckinghamshire, before becoming Senior Curate of St Mary's Lichfield. In 1889 be became Vicar of Whittington in Shropshire and then Shrawardine. He married Margaret Anne and they had two daughters. It was in 1896 he moved to Tong to be its Vicar, and while here he was a member of Shifnal District Council, the Board of Guardians, and Chairman of Shifnal Cottage Hospital. He was an accomplished writer, and a Fellow of the Royal Historical Society. His pocket book *The Churches of Shropshire* is still a useful companion when travelling around the county. He also wrote *A History of the Albrighton Hunt*, and part of the *Shrewsbury School Register*. After he left Tong Auden became Chaplain of the St John's Hospital in Lichfield before retiring, at the age of 65, to Stafford.

List of Illustrations

Acknowledgements:
I am very grateful to Mr John R. L. Smith for the pictures of the church and the church windows on the cover; to Mrs. F. Hill, Mr Mrs R. Chilton and Dr Mrs Lynn for permission to use the photos of their houses; to George and Christopher Frost for the photos of the Tong Cup, the chest, the bas-relief, the rules for the Great Bell, and the houses in Tong; to Shropshire Archives for the print from the microfiche of the churchwardens' accounts, and the drawing of the 1855 map; to Mr David Dixon and others for the loan of some of the old prints and photos which I did not already have. I have tried to acknowledge everyone's generous help, and plead for mercy should I have failed.

INDEX

This index uses the modern spelling of the words. In the original text itself various spellings are used.

Printed in the United Kingdom
by Lightning Source UK Ltd.
PP267500001B/1-2

9 781845 490102